ARTISTIC PRODUCTIVITY
AND
MENTAL HEALTH

Publication Number 592
AMERICAN LECTURES SERIES®

A Monograph in
The BANNERSTONE DIVISION *of*
AMERICAN LECTURES IN PSYCHOLOGY

Edited by
MOLLY HARROWER, Ph.D.
Professor of Research in Clinical Psychology
Department of Psychiatry
Temple University School of Medicine
Philadelphia, Pennsylvania

Artistic Productivity
and
Mental Health

Prepared under the auspices of the
Postgraduate Center for Mental Health

By

EDRITA FRIED, Ph.D.

Abby Bloomgarden, M.S.S.
William Lewis, M.D.
Ida Mermelstein, M.S.S.
Rose Spiegel, M.D.
Virginia Watts, M.S.S.

With a Foreword by
CHAIM GROSS
New York City

CHARLES C THOMAS · PUBLISHER
Springfield · Illinois · U.S.A.

Published and Distributed Throughout the World by
CHARLES C THOMAS • PUBLISHER
BANNERSTONE HOUSE
301-327 East Lawrence Avenue, Springfield, Illinois, U.S.A.
NATCHEZ PLANTATION HOUSE
735 North Atlantic Boulevard, Fort Lauderdale, Florida, U.S.A.

*With THOMAS BOOKS careful attention is given to all details of
manufacturing and design. It is the Publisher's desire to present books
that are satisfactory as to their physical qualities and artistic possibilities
and appropriate for their particular use. THOMAS BOOKS will be true
to those laws of quality that assure a good name and good will.*

Printed in the United States of America
H-2

Collaborators

ABBY BLOOMGARDEN, M.S.S.
Senior Therapist
Adult Therapy Department
Postgraduate Center for Mental Health
New York, New York

EDRITA FRIED, Ph.D.
Senior Supervising Psychologist
Postgraduate Center for Mental Health
New York, New York
Assistant Professor of Psychiatry
Albert Einstein College of Medicine
New York, New York

WILLIAM C. LEWIS, M.D.
Professor of Psychiatry
University of Wisconsin Medical School
Madison, Wisconsin

IDA MERMELSTEIN, M.S.S.
Lecturer
Supervisor
Teaching Staff
Postgraduate Center for Mental Health
New York, New York

ROSE SPIEGEL, M.D.
Supervising Analyst
Faculty Member
William Alanson White Institute
New York, New York

VIRGINIA WATTS, M.S.S.
Lecturer
Supervisor
Postgraduate Center for Mental Health
New York, New York

Foreword

PSYCHOANALYSIS and psychoanalytic psychotherapy can be of considerable help to the artist, and I find that this study gives some clear and detailed illustrations of this fact. Various mistaken ideas about productivity and the conditions conducive to it are current among artists, artists-to-be, and the general public. False notions may be harmful to the person who wants to give his life to creative activity. I frequently encounter such ideas among my students in classrooms. This book helps to clear up some of the confusion.

Some commonly-held views to the contrary, the artist has to be happy in his personal life and have peace of mind so that he can create. Turmoil, unhappy love affairs, and chaotic conditions won't let an artist go to work. I feel that if you have a good spouse half your work is done. What happens to many talented people is that when numerous things go wrong in their personal lives, they feel tempted to quit their work, and eventually they do this. Talent can get lost in unhappy marriages; or when love gets divided too drastically between work and children; or when the pressure to make a living becomes so great that it overshadows everything else. When talented people get confused in these complicated times in which we are living, they also frequently lose the ability to work.

The artist has to be an honest person. He must know how to look into himself for his own ideas and whatever drives him on. A true artist does not look to others to take on their ideas. Also, quite contrary to what a lot of people say, organization and a certain amount of order are conditions for working well as an artist. Sloppiness, chaos and disorder are not a good environment. Sometimes when I walk into a class and the model stands in the center of the room with the students placed around the model, I pass from one student to another and take a look at their stands. I might come to a neatly-dressed student, say a young woman, but her stand is cluttered, and I know that the clutter prevents her from working. I ask her, "Is your home that way?" She says, "No, my home is neat." I tell her that if her stand is cluttered and lacks some kind of harmony, then she won't get anywhere. Sculptors who are disorganized will produce disorganized work which will suffer from a lack of order.

Above all, talent means that your eyes are open and you are not blind, for the talented person sees more of the basic things than the untalented one. If talent is missing, psychoanalytic treatment will not provide it, of course. But if talent is held back, if it is prevented from asserting itself, or if any of the requirements for artistic work which I mentioned are absent, then I believe that the psychoanalyst and psychotherapist can be of great help. Some of my friends have gone into treatment, and I have noticed that they benefited a lot. I think of an artist who had been married a few times and after his last divorce started to live rather promiscuously. He was not a happy man, and his life was a big confusion. After he underwent treatment he settled down with one woman, a good woman. He resumed his work and turned out piece after piece. In fact, the colors in his paintings became more persuasive. Everything took on a brighter outlook. Similarly, most of the artists referred to in this book were helped to be more productive because they were helped in their personal lives and shown how to cope with some personality problems. Take the young woman sculptor mentioned in Case 5. Of course, I do not know her, but her story interested me very much. She was confused in her personal life, and that confusion threatened her talent, which is considerable. The story of her treatment, as it unfolds, is to me altogether credible. Treatment helped her in various ways. She got encouraged about herself as a person and as her confidence in herself unfolded, she became happier in her personal life and therefore worked more and better. In her case happiness meant finding love and companionship.

I notice that another one of the artists, who is reported in Case 4 of this book, learned how not to be pushed around so much by his wife. As he stood up to her, he became less resentful and happier. You can take the case histories one by one and see how the artists became personally happier people and had more access to the peace of mind you need to work. The artist, it stands to reason, needs peace of mind as much or more than any other working person. As to being blind and closing your eyes to the basic impressions of life and in the artistic learning situation, treatment can sometimes open a person's vision. That is also shown in Case 4. That artist was closed-minded because he was too preoccupied with inner problems. Psychoanalytic therapy cleared them away in large measure. He was a man who allowed himself to be influenced too much by others and had not yet found himself, but because of a core of talent he became better during treatment. Analytic therapy can help a person to find himself, to find his own decisions, his own memories, his own visions, his own way of viewing the world.

Inasmuch as psychotherapy helps persons to find a better order—that is, being neither chaotic nor too rigidly tidy, which isn't order in the best sense either—it helps them to acquire better work habits and thus frees and improves creativity.

In my conviction, real artists don't suffer from the problems that are commonly described as work blocks. The sheer quantity of the output of the great masters is enormous. I, myself, work long hours from morning to evening, and when I get home and relax a bit I am ready again to start sketching. I don't consider myself the exception but rather the rule. It is the sign of the dilettante to wait for the inspiration and to get up at midnight when it strikes. The muse does not touch you this way. You work as an artist just as you work in an office. You get up in the morning and you go to your studio and you put your hand on something, anything, and that will bring you back to your work. Maybe some artists give five hours to their work and others ten, but they all work with regularity. I have the impression that the psychotherapists in this study took that attitude and helped their patients to view their work in that way.

This book is beautifully written and should interest various groups of people: it will, of course, be of interest to the professional, but also to artists and to people in general. The language is easy to read and not cluttered by technical details, and many people could discover aspects of their own selves in these case histories. I enjoyed the text while I read it.

CHAIM GROSS

Preface

THE CLINICAL material and research findings reported in this study present the outcome of the so-called "Arts Project," a research undertaking sponsored by the Postgraduate Center for Mental Health. The Postgraduate Center carries out four intertwining yet differentiated functions. It serves as a training institute, provides extensive clinical services, trains mental health consultants, and carries out research. The investigation of the impact of psychotherapy upon the creative habits of artists was one of the Center's specialized projects. The original idea for the project came from the late Robert Kaufmann, himself an artist, and Walter Weiss, President of the "Arts Fund," and for seven years President of the Board of Trustees of the Post-graduate Center for Mental Health. Mr. Kaufmann and Mr. Weiss established the "Arts Fund" from which came the major original contribution to set up the Arts Project. Later, contributions were made by the Geraldine and Joseph Mindell Foundation.

Dr. Lewis R. Wolberg, Director of the Postgraduate Center and Chairman of the Arts Project Board, made comments on various versions of the manuscript which were of great help. Dr. Harvey Dain, Dr. Emanuel Schwartz, Dr. Clifford Sager, Dr. Bernard Riess, Mr. Irving Schwartz and Dr. Ralph Gundlach gave valuable time to the Arts Project Board.

The project is grateful to Dr. Rose Spiegel who carried out various functions in a creative way: she coordinated the project at its inception before I became its coordinator and served as our screening psychiatrist who skillfully ascertained facts bearing on the artistic achievements of our applicants.

Many thanks are due to the therapist-collaborators, who in addition to engaging in the psychotherapy of the artists gave generously of their time and thoughts in joint meetings devoted to consideration of specific and general questions of creativity as far as all patients were concerned. They prepared the essential statements on which the questionnaires were based and answered the long questionnaires meticulously. The therapist-collaborators, Mrs. Abby Bloomgarden, Miss Ida Mermelstein, Dr. Rose Spiegel, Mrs. Virginia Watts, and myself, were responsible for the final preparation of the respective case reports. The therapists were, without exception, selected on account of their special interest in creativity and in the treatment of artists.

Dr. Sabert Basescu assisted me in the earlier study and interpretation of data and Dr. Anthony Phillip assisted in the middle phase of research, and I wish to acknowledge their ideas and interest.

Of course the study could not have been carried out without the willingness of the artist-patients to undergo treatment within this project and to cooperate by filling in the questionnaires designed for them. Finally, I would like to thank Mrs. Ruth Marcus for her patience and help in preparing the various drafts of the manuscript.

EDRITA FRIED

New York, New York

Contents

ARTISTIC PRODUCTIVITY
AND
MENTAL HEALTH

CHAPTER 1

Connections Between Creativity and Psychopathology

For a variety of reasons felt only dimly and intuitively by the public at large and the artist in particular, the assumption has existed, perhaps for as long as we can remember, that there are connections between the ingenuity and power of creation, on the one hand, and insanity on the other. For this reason a good many creative personalities, for whom the ability to produce in their field of art supplies the essence of life, have hesitated to undergo psychoanalytic psychotherapy. Perhaps, they postulate, we need to be neurotic or psychotic in order to remain creative. As Lawrence Kubie put it (8) (*Neurotic Distortions of the Creative Process*, Porter Lectures, Series 22, University of Kansas Press, 1958): "Many psychologically ailing artists . . . including some individuals whose productivity may have been seriously injured by their neurosis, refuse therapy out of a fear that in losing illness they will lose . . . their creative zeal and spark." With this and related issues in mind we undertook this investigation. We wished to establish specifically how personality changes obtained through analytic psychotherapy would affect the artists' work. Would they be as productive after psychotherapy, or would they be more productive, and what particular changes would become evident in the work?

A primary problem was how to determine changes in the creative products. As psychotherapists and research workers we could not consider ourselves equipped—despite each participant's decisive interest in one or several fields of art—to say whether the works produced while the patient was in therapy and after treatment was ended were of a higher or lower caliber than be-

[3]

fore. Even art critics and academic experts in the field of the fine and dramatic arts have not agreed on criteria to make evaluations of this kind valid. Hence it was decided to study changes in *work habits* instead of changes in *work products*. Work habits, as we see them, are the artist's intellectual, emotional and behavioral approaches to his work. This study, then, is a report on changes in work patterns as they occurred after the artists' first nine months of psychoanalytic treatment. We observed how the work habits were affected once the artists, under the impact of psychoanalytic therapy, began to dissolve some conflicts, exchange old conflicts for newer ones, depart from regressive life habits, experience new balances between the id-ego-super-ego structures and repair specific ego-weaknesses.

Are there specific psychological mechanisms and processes, that are associated both with the creative act and the psychotic state? Indeed there are a certain number of processes and aspects of psychological functioning which exist in both conditions, but it must be added quickly that the particular use of such mechanisms and the circumstances accompanying them are quite different in the two groups. The similarities of functioning in the creative act and the neurotic or psychotic state are invariably accompanied by specific differences. The psychological process which appears pathological in the neurotic or insane person is accompanied in the creative act by other functions which result in the non-pathological product. Freud's statement that the "forces motivating the artist are the same conflicts which drive other people into neurosis" (3) (F. Deutsch: Mind, Body and Art. *Daedalus,* 89:34, 1960) is thus too general. Freud failed to specify the differences between the creative process and the pathological one.

The creative person makes something that is new, uniquely his own and that arouses—sometimes swiftly, usually only gradually—a feeling of contact in other persons. The artist himself frequently denies that this is his intention. Such denials are frequently insincere or else are made without realizing the underlying unconscious desire. For most artists, most of the time, do wish to arouse responses in other people. It is one of the tests of a work of art whether others, when exposed to it repeatedly, find their thinking and feeling expanded, enriched and accentuated. To deserve to be called a work of art, a creative product has to have a universal impact in the same sense that it affects broad groups of persons, if not immediately, then eventually. The products which psychotic persons make do not possess such universal impact. We may be able, particularly if we are trained in symbolism, to understand messages they convey, for instance that the creator is full of great anger, but though they may evoke fear or sympathy these works do not elicit responses of the enriching kind described. According to Ernst Kris (5) (*Psychoanalytic Explorations in Art,* Int. Universities Press, N.Y., N.Y. 1952) "the psychotic uses symbols which do not reverberate." As his speech is a soliloquy uttered with little or no awareness of listeners' state of receptivity, his work has an autistic cast that makes it stand out all by itself, but in a way that we describe as odd, rather than unique. The difference between the bizarreness of the psychotic and the uniqueness of the creative person can be understood clearly in the case of the actor. The actor's chief artistic tool is his own personality. Every great actor has an unusual personality. He is extraordinary. We feel that his emotions are big, or raw, that his range of feeling is especially wide and that the gestures and the use of the voice is new. He plays a great part, say that of Hamlet, as no one has played it before and this allows those who listen to have an unprecedented and moving experience. Moreover, the great actor on stage—no matter how vain he may be in private life—uses his unique personality always in the service of the part he plays. By contrast, an unusual person whose emotional and expressive resources are employed primarily towards the expression of his own whims and who is out of touch with experiences outside himself appears bizarre, not creative. The true artist is in touch both with that in himself that is unique and with the outside world. His uniqueness is employed and expressed in a manner that heightens other persons' capacity for experience and even functioning, though often after much delay.

The artists we observed were all unusual people. However,

only five of them had the universal quality just described. They could pick up and express out-of-the-ordinary notions and present them in such a way that other persons were struck by them and felt that something significant was going on. Only one person, Brendan Daltrow, the sixth patient described, was unusual without possessing an extended appeal. He was special in an odd way both in his personal life and in his work. He was the least creative of the artists and he used his powers and time primarily to elaborate on his pathology rather than to create products with universal appeal.

The artist draws on his conscious, his preconscious and his unconscious when he creates, Lawrence Kubie (3) (. . . *ibid.*) has emphasized that the preconscious processes are the raw material out of which artistic products are created. When he says that the "forms and patterns which play upon our preconscious perceptual processes incessantly from earliest infancy on shape our creative responses without our knowledge," he presumes implicitly and correctly that a special receptivity to such impressions on the preconscious is a prerequisite for creativity. Vulnerability, or a state of being not too heavily protected by various mechanisms and manoeuvres of defense, is indeed a requirement for the creative personality and for that matter in the intellectual elite, the group to which Gerald Sykes refers as "the Hidden Remnant" (10) (Gerald Sykes: *The Hidden Remnant,* Harper and Brothers, 1962, p 16). We will see that several of our artists who used obsessive-compulsive defense mechanisms—Cases 1, 2, and 6—were considerably more creative when analytic psychotherapy reduced their rigid defenses than when these defenses were employed broadly. The fact that three of the six persons on whom we report were so heavily defended points out some flaw in the screening procedures used, for it would have been indicated to select through appropriate screening persons with broader mood swings and less entrenched defenses.

If the artist is vulnerable by the above definition so, too, is the borderline personality and the schizophrenic, whose defenses are erratic, brittle and often narrow in range. Again we are faced with a similarity in personality structure and functioning.

Yet the difference in functioning is just as important. The artist's vulnerability exposes him to his internal and to the external world permitting both to make deep marks on him *which he then projects on his art.* The schizophrenic and psychotic who does not function as an artist fails to externalize in creative work the marks that are made. Often, to be sure, this is pure coincidence. Had the person with psychological illness learned the availability and the skills of creative expression he might turn towards communication through art and possibly to communications with some universal significance. Indeed Art Therapy as practiced by Naumburg (8) (Naumburg, Margaret: ——) and others attempts to encourage externalizations of a similar kind, thus making narrower, in a certain sense, the gap between artist and mental sufferer. It is possible that the artist inherently, that is congenitally, possesses an ego that leaves the psychic apparatus particularly vulnerable to stimulation and that has a lower than average threshold for it. The person burdened by severe psychopathology is similarly invaded too easily by stimulation. The question arises whether this condition changes in therapy and whether if it changes the creative patterns are bound to change. Here our facts shall supply an answer. In the case of Vincent van Gogh, whose psychological functioning was deduced from his letters by Joost Meerloo (7), shows an artist destroyed by his vulnerability. For van Gogh painting represented a means of salvation from the pains which the avalanche of stimuli that trespassed the low threshold of his ego inflicted. When he painted he could bind the profusion of stimuli, when he was restrained from painting the stimuli as well as his own aggression overwhelmed him.

Another reason for the frequently drawn parallel between artist and maniac is the narcissism present in high degree in both. Both categories of people have a great energy investment in themselves and what springs from the self. It is not a new fact that object relations, namely relations to those closest, such as parents, siblings, wife and offspring, as well as to people that are more distant, usually are disturbed both in the life of the emotionally deeply disturbed person and in the artist. Certainly this was true of the artists who were treated in the project on which we shall report. In fact the majority of those treated were motivated for psychotherapy by the very fact that their relationships, both intimate and casual, were poor. Thus the question arises whether the artist who through psychotherapy becomes able to sustain more stable and tranquil relationships with the persons around him is willing to invest as much energy in his work. The data collected will supply a yes answer to this query. Our artists, once they began investing more energy in other people, still had enough left over for their work.

Another psychological faculty toward which both the artist and the mentally disturbed veer is ease in regression. In regression the vigilance of the ordering, administering ego or rational mind is suspended and the domaine of the instincts, the unfettered roaming of the emotions, preconscious thinking, and primary process functioning have the upper hand. The proposition laid down by Kris (ibid.) (Kris, Ernst: that the creative act rests upon a regression in the service of the ego is not questioned by any school of psychoanalytic thinking. But as the definition by Kris tells us, the regression of the artist is different from that of the person who is insane. The artist wills his regression and while it takes place the ego is standing on the sideline observant of and receptive to the processes that stream from the primitive, intuitive part of the personality, the id. There is in the artist, as Bellak points out (ibid.), (Bellak, Leo: Creativity, Some Random Notes to a Systematic Consideration, *Journal of Projective Techniques, 22*: No. 4, 1958) an oscillation between the id and the ego, between the primitive and unfettered mind, on the one hand, and the administrative realm, on the other. This oscillation makes it possible for the rational and ordering mind to catch a great deal of what erupts from the imaginative mind. In contrast to this kind of regression the psychotic surrenders entirely to the regressive process. He cannot will its beginning, as can the artist, who usually works on a schedule, and he cannot with another part of himself stand by and capture what comes out of the unbound id. Where the ego of the artist lurks in the background and intercepts the envisaged creations, shaping them and making them enduring, the ego of the insane person cannot be relied upon to perform such tasks. It is entirely or partially out of commission, rather inactive and often too chaotic to go through the ordering activities that must be undertaken if the erupted id material is to assume the purposefulness of a work of art. The insane ego is often too impatient to acquire or execute the skills that in the artistic act must be applied to ideas, to form, to erupted experience, making art through blending many kinds of content with many kinds of materials, colors, glazes, tactile effects, or, in the case of the writer, skillful and fine verbal selections and structures. And finally, the ego of the insane person does not possess the ability to insure that the final product is both highly individualistic and yet has some universally valid significance.

One can think of another constellation which is responsible for the confusion between creativeness and pathology. While truly creative work is a most demanding activity in terms of self-discipline and exposure to emotional stress, work that is quasi-creative can be relatively easy on the emotions and the ego. Thus is happens that a good many unstable persons who are not genuinely ready or willing to cope with the demands of either the everyday or the artistic world take refuge in the field of art. They are often referred to as the Bohemians. Whether such persons know it or not, they use art as an excuse to keep irregular hours and to waste time. Art helps them justify the fact that they haven't made headway in the world, since they can include themselves without reckoning among the many artists who were misunderstood in their own time. They can write or paint in a pretend way, often not even clear to themselves. The fact that their artistic products do not find a market can be explained as the result of the ignorance and insensitivity of dealers, agents, etc. The presence of such a nucleus of refugees from the harsh everyday world for which their psychic functioning does not equip them because they are disturbed has contributed to the notion that the artistic world is full of disturbed people.

CHAPTER 2

Methods of Observation*

To study some of the connections between Creativity and Psychopathology a Research Project called the Arts Project was undertaken by the Postgraduate Center for Psychotherapy. On the basis of data obtained from the treatment in three times a week analytic psychotherapy of our artist patients, we attempted to evaluate the relationship between changes in personality and changes in the artists' creative work habits. Each artist was observed and data were collected for at least three years. Thus the findings presented cover the results obtained in the beginning and middle phase of therapy. While nearly all artists remained in treatment beyond the three years, observations could not be continued because funds were limited to the two-and-a-half-year period.

At the inception we had to ask ourselves who should be considered a creative artist for purposes of the study. We decided that painters, sculptors, writers, composers and performing musicians, and actors, who gave their full time to creative work were to be included. Commercial artists were excluded. In selecting patients, the age limits were held roughly between twenty-five and fifty. It was felt that those younger had not yet had a chance to work extensively in their field, and that those who were older would present too rigid personality structures and work habits to be modified optimally through psychotherapy. Altogether we treated twelve individuals engaged in different branches of the creative arts.

Only persons who had achieved a considerable degree of

---

*Dr. Anthony Phillip, who is mentioned in the Foreword, collaborated with the author in preparing this chapter.

artistic expression and technical skill were considered. Artistic caliber was assessed in three ways: 1) we noted the level of galleries and exhibitions where the painters and sculptors showed their work; the stature and artistic integrity of institutions that gave a hearing to the performing musicians and composers; the quality of the publishers, publications and radio and television programs where the work of the writers was presented, and the level of the theatrical productions in which the actors appeared. 2) We secured opinions from persons of recognized stature and judgment in the various fields, such as outstanding artists, composers, museum directors, etc. Their advice was sought in order to exclude amateurs or persons lacking in talent and accomplishment. 3) The director of the project, and the screening psychiatrist, after making their decisions on candidates, jointly discussed the individuals selected with the professional Board of the Arts Project. Available data was once more scrutinized and the final decisions made. Careful as this procedure was, it did not insure full success. Four of the twelve individuals admitted proved not to possess the desired caliber and were not sufficiently serious about the treatment offered them. Two of the four dropped out. The records of the other two were excluded from the final study. A fifth candidate obtained important engagements abroad and left treatment to go to Europe. In a sixth case the therapist did not provide sufficiently extensive records to follow specific developments of the case. Thus, while we carried altogether twelve creative individuals as patients, we were left with six complete cases on which to report.

One of the important decisions at the outset of the project concerned the size of the sample. Should the project focus on a larger sample, provide shorter treatment and present a survey-type report or concentrate on a smaller number of patients, who could be treated more extensively and observed in depth? The latter alternative was chosen. The project was one of the first of its kind. Because of the pilot nature of the study, it was assumed that the best service would lie in testing certain assumptions, and establishing some preliminary findings. These assumptions, hypotheses, and findings from a small group of creative individuals could then be tested and verified on a larger sample.

Let us for purposes of illustration bring in some of the preliminary findings which will be documented in the following chapters.

1) Of the six creative individuals on whom we shall report, five (namely the Cases 1, 2, 3, 4, and 6) changed notably. Personality difficulties such as excessive passivity, apathy, depression, despair, low self-esteem, frictions with close figures, etc., lessened considerably and the changes seem to be based on deep reconstructions of the personality structure.

2) Concurrently with the changes in personality, creative work habits, or the work patterns as they are called here, changed for the better. The changes were always comprehensive, that is to say all work patterns improved, though in different degrees, as the ratings given to the various directions of development show. As to Case 5, interestingly enough the patient, whose ego strength was quite limited, changed only moderately during the three years during which he was observed in the project. However, after he terminated treatment—he continued treatment for two years following termination of the project—he established himself effectively as an actor. He achieved satisfaction and acclaim, and his personal life improved notably beyond the degree noted in the observation period.

In all cases the changes in work patterns appeared connected with the personality changes in a manner usually foretold in the predictions which were made in the ninth month of treatment. Of the five artists whose development was quite marked four (Cases 1, 2, 4 and 6) had considerable work difficulties prior to therapy. All of them became much more able to work in the sense that they did not need chemical stimulants to get started, spent far less time inactive or in preliminary time-consuming stalling, and noted a greater fluidity in their work habits as well as other changes that are going to be specified. Case 3, who had no working difficulties when treatment started, remained productive throughout therapy. Future studies made in a survey manner with larger number of artist subjects could set out to verify on a bigger sample some of the connections which we found between personality problems and work problems and dissolutions of personality problems and abolition of work problems. For instance, how many other painters become more fluid if their aggression is freed, as was the case with artists 1, 2, 4, and 6? How many creative persons work more easily when omnipotent fantasies are dissolved as was the case with artists 1, 2, 4, 5 and 6.

3) The predictions that were made by the therapists in consultation with research in the ninth month of treatment had the following double purposes: a) The predictions set forth the connection which was understood to exist between personality problem and work problem. One of the ways we have of confirming our assumptions of certain connections between personality factors and certain characteristics of the work patterns are the predictions. The predictions stated causal effects between certain aspects of personality structure and certain work patterns. The therapist worked not with work patterns but with personality structure. Hence there is good reason to assume that if certain personality changes were indeed followed by the predicted work pattern changes a cause effect connection existed between the two. Actually 87 percent of the predicted effects of personality change upon work pattern change did take place, according to questionnaires and ratings along directions of development. Thirteen percent of the predicted changes did not come through. b) Since we wished to obtain some measurement of therapeutic success with regard to personality structure and work patterns, we decided to use the so-called directions of development. These were envisaged roads of change, intended courses of development towards which the therapeutic work from the ninth month of treatment on was geared. The therapists at that time, together with research, noted the dynamic structure of each patient and together formulated various directions of development along which the therapeutic work was expected to progress. According to the degree to which progress was made ratings were assigned by outside raters to movement along the directions of development. Directions were set down for personality changes and for connected, interrelated work pattern changes which were envisaged and expected as a by-product of the change in personality structure. The fact that the predictions came true in large measure shows that it is indeed possible to plan the therapeutic movement in such a way

that directions of change can be formulated and ratings along such dimensions be assigned meaningfully.

Theoretical Assumptions

To ascertain how psychoanalytic psychotherapy affects the creative individual, a number of working assumptions were made.

Assumption Number 1

To assess the effect of psychotherapy on the work of the creative individual, we must first establish its effect on the personality of the patient, that is, on the totality of psychic processes by which the individual makes his adaptation to life situations. Stated in operational terms, this means:*what changes in needs, ego functions, defenses and other adaptive modes have occurred?* The reason for using this working assumption is the factor that prompted the artist patient to seek treatment. The majority of our artist patients sought therapeutic intervention not because there existed interferences with their creativity, although such interferences usually existed. Rather they came to treatment because they suffered from severe disturbances in their personal lives. They had sexual difficulties, they were in the grips of anxiety states, there were severe frictions with mates and/or colleagues which made life miserable and propelled them to seek help. *To the patients, their personal experiences were of central importance. This is where they sought change.* While the creative aspects of life were invariably touched upon and usually altered, this constituted primarily an end result of work with other personality segments.

Assumption Number 2

We assumed that the psychotherapist, even when himself artistically active or artistically experienced in other ways, is not qualified professionally to make judgments about the creative products *per se* nor about changes in the creative products. *What he can observe and evaluate as a psychotherapist* is the artist's approach to his work, his work habits or creative patterns: behavioral changes in this area represent observable data and can be reported on.

Therefore, sticking to operational terms we asked: *what changes in work habits have occurred?* In our focus on work habits we felt we were getting as close to the creative process as possible, considering that one of our over-riding aims was to leave the analytic situation inviolate and unchanged by our research needs. Work habits rather than finished creative works were studied. Assessment of artistic products involves the use of independent *artist* judges, and presented an extension of the project for which we were not prepared at that point.* We were interested in the *creative process* more than in the *created product.*

Assumption Number 3

We assumed that changes in the personality will be related to changes in the dynamics of the creative process. Changes in the latter were assumed to be a consequence of the former. There is a parallel between the more comprehensive ego functions which a person uses in adapting to physical processes within the organism and to the environment in general and 'the more specific functions called for in the creative process. To sum up: we studied changes in dynamics, particularly in ego functions, on the one hand, and changes in work patterns, on the other. Then we assumed that there exist certain specific connections between the change along the dimension of hostility in general and the diminishing of the created product, specifically.

Our assumption that therapeutic experiences which touch the personality and produce genuine changes in dynamics will lead to parallel changes in creative patterns proved true.

Assumption Number 4

The variables existing in each case were numerous. Moreover they differed from case to case. The array of defenses, the nature of the ego functions and their specific combinations, patterning and structural inter-relationships varied from one patient to

---

*Dr. Sabert Basescu, research assistant during the early phase of the project, consistently advocated periodic evaluations of creative products by experts. This idea was attempted but proved too complex a task to be carried out.

another. We concluded that in order to make valid observations concerning the effect of psychotherapy, each case had to be studied separately, as a "microcosm" or "entity" in its own right, with a custom-made set of measurements. Specifically this meant that our prime research tool, a set of detailed questionnaires, had to differ from case to case to "catch" the dynamics of each patient.

The Questionnaire

The questionnaires comprise the "meat" of our data and as such warrant detailed consideration. They were prepared as follows: After approximately nine months of treatment, and after consultation with the coordinator of the project and members of the research staff, the therapist prepared an exhaustive summary of the patient's dynamics, defense system, character structure, symptomatology and work patterns. On the basis of this, plus the process recordings of sessions for these first months of therapy, the two-part questionnaire was constructed. During this preparation two guiding principles were kept in mind:

1) *Both the construction and the answering of the questionnaire should be spread among as many people as possible in order to minimize bias.* The project director and her assistant, not the therapist, prepared the questionnaires—one for the therapist to answer, and one for the patient. The fact that two separate questionnaires were answered by two separate people reduced bias to some degree. Two evaluations of progress were made. Evaluation of changes in dynamics was derived from the therapist's responses, and changes in creative work habits were observed from the patient's answers. Thus a comparison of different types of progress was based on separate sources of data that were not directly related.

This method is founded on the scientific principle that the measurement of a phenomenon is not necessarily undertaken most advantageously by studying the phenomenon itself. Rather one can describe the phenomenon under study by noting the effect it has upon some other related phenomenon. We know that mercury contracts or expands depending on the quantity of heat: we measure temperature not by observing it directly but by noting its effect on a column of mercury.

2) Our second principle was to ask the kind of questions that would help both therapists and patients to report on the therapeutic experience in concrete fashion. The questionnaires presented specific questions in operational terms, and called for discreet and particular answers. This does not mean that we asked only for externalized, measurable behavior. On the contrary, we included such manifestations as thoughts, reports of physical sensations such as joyous feelings, palpitations, fantasies, a wish not to think of someone, and so on. In short, as long as specific information was reported as contrasted with some global intuitive experience of either therapist or patient, statements reflecting physical, mental or emotional states were acceptable. We did not inquire, for example, about the current status of a patient's passive dependence in "open-ended" fashion, such as, "tell us how the passive-dependent attitude has changed." Rather in a case where the patient's passivity appeared to be pathological, the therapist's questionnaire included questions such as these:

> Give specific illustrations of the patient's self image during the past four months.
> When frustrated did the patient remain depressed and inactive? If not, what activities, mental (plans, concrete projects, sharp clarifications, etc.) and physical did he undertake?
> What were the urinary patterns specifically? (In this case the patient urinates frequently during periods of passivity and becomes more intensely aware of the quantities of urine expelled.)

Specific questions like the above were repeated after four months, and again drew specific answers that enabled us to evaluate change.

Questionnaire #1: Submitted to patient J.N.

(Period: April 1, 1958 - Oct. 1, 1958)*

THERAPIST: DR. B.C.

During your treatment you have brought out certain habits, successes and difficulties concerning your work. Please answer these questions that deal specifically with your situation as a creative person. In your answers consider how you felt about your work in the last three months.

1. *How much time have you been able to give to your painting?*

Only recently have I been finding more time for work. This wouldn't be a fair evaluation of the results of therapy since until this date I have been greatly involved with the setting up and the arrangements of a new studio next to my home. Even without therapy, the physical setup of our new home should offer more opportunity for work time since it eliminates about two hours of daily travelling time from my previous home to my studio. In addition, however, the studio next to my living quarters permits me to go down to work whenever I have a free hour. There has been an actual increase in the desire to work!

2. *How do you concentrate on your work?*

Very well, but the lack of a consistent day-to-day schedule of work interferes with a consistent train of thought and carry-through of projects that were begun.

3. *Do you work through a whole canvas or do you work on individual segments of it?*

I believe that this question refers to my statement that paintings often failed to resolve themselves until I had courageously broken through a particular passage that I held on to and worked around because I believed it to be effective. The fear of losing the supposed effective area prevented the achievement of a total unity in the painting construction. This concern for a specific passage and holding on to this passage is not as prevalent now.

4. *Tell us specifically about your individual style, please.*

Most painters have an individual and consistent manner of painting—what then occurs to Mr. Picasso who paints in many manners and styles and still his work is recognizable as individual. Though I do seem to work in various manners—or approaches, never has the variance been so great that people who know my work would not be able to identify me with the work. It is true that the work even now does not have what

---

*Treatment was interrupted during the summer months. The months covered are: April, May, June, September.

might be referred to as a trade-mark. Though my work is and can be identified with me, there are those that have frowned and sit waiting for my settling down to a particular manner. In careful self search, I have often wondered if the possibility of really breaking bonds and smashing through the need to conform to a mild kind of non-conformism and perhaps work in a manner that would leave me alone without any prop of acceptance—or perhaps this radical change would win adherents after its first shock. To return to a more specific answer to this question—let me state that my work has been moving into an area of richer color and a lighter key. I cannot answer the question more specifically until I have completed more work. I am certain that there are break throughs of new qualities that seem to appear and vanish again.

5. *How often do you paint over practically completed paintings? Would you please compare the present situation with previous phases.*
The answer is I frequently paint over completed paintings. But the paintings I have worked over were old ones (three years ago.) Recently I worked over a new and completed painting on a day when I was disturbed by a family problem. After an hour or two of unsuccessful effort I left it unfinished and unresolved and quit painting for the rest of the day. In the process of making the changes I felt so unsuccessful that it increased my sense of feeling disturbed.

6. *What has your feeling about your work been, specifically with regard to a sense of freedom in your work?*
I feel happier in my work. I feel more confident. I feel that I want to work. I feel certain that with therapy and working time, there is happiness available in abundance.

7. *Have you utilized new forms in your work?*
I cannot answer this question yet. I need to do more work —there are indications of break throughs.

8. *You've mentioned your concern with balance and symmetry in your work. What has been happening with this aspect of your painting?*
I do not recall speaking of a concern with balance in my work. In referring to *balance* it was in general reference to life and living on a theoretical basis which would include reference to a theory in relation to painting.

9. *You have mentioned that your paintings were ponderous and awkward. How do you feel about this now?*
I do not feel that way about my present works. I feel a definite kind of graceful flow in the work except in the break through of new forms which look awkward.

10. *How have your paintings sold lately?*
In the past year I have sold less than in previous years. My paintings never have been sold to strangers at the gallery except in rare occasions. This past year cannot be judged accurately in this area due to my preoccupation with the new house.

Questionnaire #2: Submitted to patient J.N.
(Period: October 1, 1958 - February 1, 1959)
THERAPIST: DR. B.C.

1. *How much time have you been able to give to your painting?*
I cannot accurately say that the amount of time I have been able to give to my work has increased but can definitely state that the aspect of time is no longer a spectre that haunts me and at the same time is elusive.

2. *How do you concentrate on your work?*
My work in the past three months centered around a series of drawings which are presently on exhibit at the H———— Galleries. These drawings are direct pen and ink drawings which required a total sense of tranquility and concentration during the production of each drawing. The technique used required precision coupled with spontaneity.

3. *Do you work through a whole canvas or do you work on individual segments of it?*
I concentrate on the canvas as a whole.

4. *Tell us specifically about your individual style, please.*
I feel that the recently completed set of drawings are completely individual in style. (By that I mean that they cannot be identified or related to some style of another artist.)

5. *How often do you paint over practically completed paintings?*
In the past three months I have not done very much painting and therefore cannot answer the question completely. There are two different ways of painting over practically completed

paintings. One way would be to paint over an almost finished canvas with a totally different concept; the other way would be to fearlessly make sweeping changes in an almost completed painting for a richer statement of the same concept. I still maintain the latter mentioned approach which I (correctly or incorrectly) believe to help me to obtain a superior effectiveness.

6. *What has your feeling about your work been, specfically with regard to a sense of freedom in your work?*
I feel freer in my work. The series of drawings, though confined to a similar manner flowed out with comparative ease. Strangely, viewers seem to be impressed with what appears to them a painstaking effort, while in reality they were extremely spontaneous efforts coupled with loving care. In my painting I feel I have already touched a newer level of freedom but I have yet to find out what will develop now that I have completed my series of drawings.

7. *Have you utilized new forms in your work?*
To a certain extent this question is coupled with the one above. Feeling freer would naturally tend to give one greater opportunity to attempt to utilize new forms. In my latest paintings new forms are beginning to evolve. I have been able to break out of the constant world of chiaroscuro (light and shade) and to use it at my choice and not be totally dependent on it. This is a break through that has developed in the past six or eight months.

8. *You've mentioned your concern with balance and symmetry in your work. What has been happening with this aspect of your painting?*
I still feel that a great creative expression is one that possesses a sense of balance just as all in nature seems to possess a quality of balance. This balance in painting could exist in all its elements, area, color, design, concept, etc. The elementary problems of balance in a painting such as area, color, texture are academic ones that can be learned and practiced but are only of value when possessed by the *artist*. The artist being one able to integrate the form with the content (so that, too, is a total unit created by balance).

9. *You have mentioned that your paintings were ponderous and awkward. How do you feel about this?*

I can only say that the drawings flow rhythmically and grace-
fully to the point (now) of almost a loss of ruggedness. (Balance! Balance!) In my paintings, also, I seem to enjoy a loss
of awkwardness.

10. *How have your paintings sold lately?*
My exhibit which opened last week and still has two weeks
to go has to date sold . . . of the . . . drawings displayed . . .
This may sound better than it really is financially, since
drawings do not command much of a price and after the cost
of framing, commissions and publicity not much is left even
if the entire exhibit was sold out. I believe that I have been
managing with the sales but deeply regret that the sales do
not manage out of the total recognition of the quality of the
aesthetic effort other than a social type of management.
I briefly wish to comment that at present I have a greater
inner security of my ability to accomplish than I have ever
had before, for which I am grateful, and which I should like
to continue to nourish and develop.

Evaluation of Questionnaire Data

The questionnaire data were evaluated by two independent
judges who used the following devices: 1) a set of *Directions
of Development* (we shall describe what is meant by this term),
and 2) a rating scheme ranging from one to nine. We rated the
progression of change as far as dynamics were concerned and
the changes as far as the creative patterns were concerned, and
compared the two sets of results.

We needed the concept of *directions of development* to rate
a forward movement with regard to dynamics and creative patterns. In order to evaluate changes in dynamics and work patterns, we needed a conceptual model of what constitutes healthy,
desirable change within a particular area. Personal growth within one area of experience does not consist, as a rule, of a forward movement along a one-dimensional continuum. Rather
change in one area takes on a complex structure along various
overlapping and differing continua.

To illustrate let us look at work with dependency needs,
which, for instance, might follow a course like this. First the
patient may not recognize his dependency at all ("I don't need

anybody to help me"); in time he may express them at the fantasy level (fantasies that powerful people extend help), still later in treatment he may express them at the level of actually seeking out competent personalities to help him, and finally he will secure gratifications by his own skills. In this case the improvement is from unconscious need to conscious need, to fantasy expression, to action that makes possible the leaning on others, to self-directed action. Such a sequence of changes within an area of experience, envisaged by the therapist, and more or less planfully pursued in treatment, is called in this project a *Direction of Development.*

Instead of rating the dependency need as existing in a lesser or in a higher degree, we consider the qualitative and structural aspects of change by defining a particular direction of development. This makes it possible for the tabulator to do justice to the topographical factor which exists in most improvements brought about through analytic psychotherapy. For instance, to give another example, let us consider Case 5. Here the therapist had to deal centrally with the homosexual problem of the patient. At times during treatment the homosexual behavior was more frequent than in the beginning. Yet the ratings of changes within the area of the sexual problem went up. The Direction of Development envisaged and pursued by the therapist and noted by research was: homosexual passivity and fantasy living —breakthrough of the aggressive drive—heightened sexual activity—heterosexuality. Hence occasional intensifications of homosexual activity were considered as part of a forward movement.

The Directions of Development were established as follows. The researcher took the major areas covered by the questionnaire and attempted to discern the path of change in each area, as the therapist appeared to contemplate it. Then, the Directions of Development were formulated—usually, though not invariably, about fifteen in the field of dynamics of personality, and seven or eight in the area of creative patterns. Then a discussion was held with the therapist. When agreement was reached on the

---

*The suggestion to resort to this kind of concept was made by Professor Robert Holt, Research Center for Mental Health, New York University.

contemplated Directions of Development, two independent judges rated changes within these Directions of Development along a nine-point scale. The arithmetic mean between the two ratings was used as the final rating. At first we applied a five-point scale but did not find it sufficiently sensitive. A rating of one was assigned to the position which the patient assumed in the beginning of treatment within the particular area which the Direction of Development covered. Put another way, the first questionnaire filled in by the therapist represented the baseline against which change was evaluated. The patient questionnaires were handled in the same way.

The Use of Predictions

About nine months after treatment began all therapists were requested to put down in writing their predictions as to how the specific creative patterns of each individual would change, if specific envisaged changes in the dynamic picture were to be obtained. To illustrate, the following are predictions from one case.

Prediction #1

If and when the autistic character orientation is reduced, the patient will have less difficulty in starting day by day to work creatively. Working hours will be more regular. Lapses of time when the patient cannot work at all will be shorter. At the same time excited work flings (with much drinking)—the patient working for twenty hours or more at a stretch—will occur less frequently. Creativity will not diminish when autism recedes. The use of visual images as a form of communication is so basic and primary and so pleasurable during the less autistic periods, that the patient is expected to always retain a strong desire to use visual imaginative expression.

Results: *While the patient indeed gave up the frenzied, extended work flings accompanied by drinking, the difficulties in getting started day by day still exist. Indeed, creativity did not diminish—and during therapy the patient acquired an eminent status in the art world.*

Prediction #2

At present the patient can work only when a state of chaos exists both in personal appearance and in the immediate work surroundings. This factor, in turn, acts as a depressant in that it is perceived by the artist as a concrete demonstration of what she considers her personal insanity. When a true inner order emerges, the obsessive compulsive defenses, which at present are at work and have to be shattered through chaotic outbreaks, will gradually be abandoned. The patient will then be able to work well regardless of bodily or environmental conditions. Forms and color arrangements will probably become more varied, and the artist's enormous imaginativeness will find full expression.

Results: *This prediction came true.*

Prediction #3

When the need for omnipotence is reduced the works will vary more in size, and oversized works will no longer be dominant. Fewer works which appear short of perfection will be destroyed. The conflict over showing and not showing creative products, which at present throws the patient into states of depression and rage, will lessen.

Results: *Large works still predominate. The artist says, however, that the motivation for creating them flows out of artistic themes rather than from an inner force impelling towards more massive efforts. Some works are still destroyed, but in a less impulsive, less furious manner. Many are, however, preserved. The artist has shown works frequently and quite freely in the past years.*

Prediction #4

Hostility is extraordinarily intense and prevailing, and has to be reduced. It is partially a defense against feelings of love or success which quickly lead to a threatening sense of disintegration. Better ego boundaries have to be established. When hostility is reduced several changes in work patterns can be expected. The cruel, jagged forms will give way to new shapes. The dark colors appearing everywhere—in dress, in living quarters and in work—will not prevail. The patient will cease to destroy artistic works. There will be fewer ruptures in relations with significant persons, and the artist's damaging dependency on Mr. F., who now functions as sole critic and sole emotional support, will be reduced.

Results: *The forms changed markedly. The prevalence of dark shades disappeared. The patient still destroys some works. The dependency on Mr. F. has disappeared, and the sinister connections with him have been completely severed.*

Illustrative Material—Two Sample Questionnaires

Questionnaire #1: Submitted to therapist

(Period: April 1, 1958 - October 1, 1958)

PATIENT: MR. X

THERAPIST: DR. Y

This questionnaire is administered at four-month intervals. The therapist receives his questionnaire before the patient does, fills it in and returns it. The patient answers his questionnaire independently.

An outline of your patient's pathology has been extrapolated from the summary statement you submitted. This outline forms the basis of the following questions which are designed to elicit a *behavioral* description of the patient's current functioning.

1. *Give specific illustrations of the patient's self image.*

Always sees two sides to everything—has never had conscious hate for anyone—if has distaste can see good qualities too. Dislikes teaching amateurs painting—doesn't feel like painter —but social worker—handmaiden to struggling students. On the other hand who is he to indulge himself in likes or dislikes. Most people work at jobs they dislike. Still an artist must have a certain amount of egocentricism.

No awkward embarrassment with large groups of people— lectures, teachers.

2. *What is the patient's behavior in relation to his wife like?*

Patient says he has arrived at shocking conclusion there are many things that wife doesn't like about him.

An ever-recurring problem—wife is constantly demanding warmth and attention—always placing him on defensive and making him feel guilty. Criticizes his frequency of sexual needs —makes him feel he is "using her"—that he is making demands on her.

After extreme provocation—left home—cried—returned home, found wife acting as though nothing had occurred—in fact air feels cleared for her and she is usually very industrious following scenes.

Mother used to complain he never responded to her requests —wife has same current complaint—that his sexual desires are in turn looked upon as demands are confusing to him.

3. *What is his behavior in relation to his colleagues?*
Fellow artists somehow have the impression he doesn't produce enough—can't change this impression though has had four one-man shows. A patronizing criticism places him in a passive position.

4. *What is his relation to therapist?*
At least three dreams during April of therapist or some authority figure watching him, peering at him.
In a dream, therapist is a sweet person who suddenly becomes sensuous, grabs him by the balls, holds him suspended up in the air and renders him powerless.

5. *How does he react to the exploitation of or injustice to others?*
Dream—daughter tells father he interferes with her. Wife says you deserve this. You don't handle her properly.
Not passive—secures sufficient ego satisfaction and adequacy in dealing with new house.
Sees as his goal in analysis to gain sufficient strength (from therapist) so as to withstand injustice and frustration—A dream makes him feel his defenses are being shaken down.
Under pressure of success-aggression at getting new house— feelings of injustice and betrayal are revived and intensified —injustice now revolves around family's lack of appreciation of how much work he does, how earnestly he works, how he places home responsibilities above all.

6. *How does he deal with his dependency needs (how is illness used?)*
Insulin injections are felt as injections of strength when he feels anxious.

7. *What are the artist's relationships to professional colleagues?*

He will praise and admire other artists' work—though they regard it as a weakness in him to do this.

Couldn't compete with F.K.'s fluidity. His paintings on same subject were complaints and observation whereas K. expressed indignation.

He is not a virtuoso in his paintings as some of his colleagues are—feels there is an awkwardness that must be concealed by great effort.

8. *What expectations does the artist have of his work?*
No answer.

9. *What are the artist's attitudes toward exhibition or sale of his paintings?*
Shame at selling paintings on social basis—can't compete with other painters in this way.

Feels hasn't enough self-regard therefore can't sell his paintings.

In selling paintings—feeling of this is *me* makes it difficult for him to sell paintings.

10. *Tell some of the patient's dreams in this period.*
A dream of painter D.H.—patient has his genitals exposed, D.H. comments how small his penis is—patient does not feel too badly. Can take criticism from D.H.—associates that D.H. criticized a painting of his when another artist was present— feels D.H. is competitive with all artists—that most artists are —he, however, does not feel this competitiveness.

11. *Tell some of the patient's fantasies.*
For first time played poker and didn't mind other players' desire to win—He used to lose interest in game as soon as others would indicate too great a desire to win.

Has always set up imaginary goals which have failed. By 1951 he was to have won the Guggenheim award but realized he couldn't compete with the politics that went on. A new symbol of achievement and eventual source of security in the house he is buying, feels anxious it may fall through.

12. *Give specific illustrations of the patient's expression of hostility toward the cousin and mother.*
Finds can now express conscious resentment toward mother.

The vindication of attaining cousin's admiration at present.

Cousin is a moralist—set up controls in his sexual life—mustn't masturbate—read graphic literature, etc.

13. Give illustrations of masochistic behavior and feeling.
Feels a stoniness, a weight on his heart in relation to the constant quarrels between himself and wife.
Following above dream and on outburst of rage toward wife —patient has several dreams of identification with father— about this time patient develops asthma-like attacks. Talks to mother, says he has his father's asthma.
Patient says of his asthma—when he had diabetes (now very minor)—he was as healthy as anyone as long as he had insulin injections but with asthma he must think of himself as an invalid—who must of necessity limit his rushing around, any scenes which will provoke him and excite him, etc.

14. How does his hostility show in his art?
Thinks of creating new forms as—"Breaking accepted forms —can't seem to go as far as to destroy the concept of the human image—must be prepared to destroy the structure he has thus far created."
Always said of his paintings that he painted in a low key— he could never see this—now with contrast of warm, bright colors, sees this.
So upset by wife's attack of him as inadequate father to daughter—angry—frustrated—went to studio—took out painting of two men, one behind bars, one with wine and loaf of bread, realized these figures must be himself. Went to another painting of woman reading in bed—realized it was wife, and wanted to throw stone at it—didn't have courage, instead painted over and over until painted out entire painting although it was painting he had admired.
Used to paint social scenes of violence, realizing this was outlet for him—now no outlet in this or elsewhere. Despite his violent feelings, there is a gentleness in his art.

15. Does hostility appear in fantasy?
Has never had aggressive fantasies toward anyone.

16. How does hostility appear in patient's dreams?
Dream—of patient's cousin and daughter—cousin was a lawyer in courtroom scene, daughter harangues the court—a bullet grazes patient, but no one pays attention to him.
Painter D.H. criticizes his paintings—in dreams criticizes the size of his genitals. Women in dreams—make him powerless and attack him sexually. In another dream, women give

strength and change to beggars. Patient at mercy of women for strength.

In dream preoccupied talking to wife driving car—turned corner—almost killed a policeman who told him, "can't you see there are new rules"—had to tell story to judge as though he had committed a major crime—somehow feels his crimes are major ones, not minor.

A dream in which patient is handed a stick and, with a cousin of his, beats up two men. Patient associated that in childhood he would be over-whelmed with rage and had to hold himself back.

17. *Does hostility affect the sexual relationships?*
Experience with girl in Europe was experienced as breaking through moral codes—wife complains about his constant sexual demands—since male should be aggressor, what should he do when he is denied—Reaction is anger, feeling of rejection. Practices withdrawal—wife will not use contraception or permit him to.

Depressions in reaction to quarrels with wife seem of shorter intensity and duration.

Patient is accused by wife of lack of warmth. A cheerlessness in the home, as being used sexually. His one memory of complete harmony is before he married and lived with fellow artist who later died.

Following scene—anger—wants to do violence to wife—instead they have sexual intercourse reassuring to both of them.

18. *Please describe the psychosomatic ailments (fatigue, asthma, hay fever, others.)*
Backache occurs in session—dream—cousin associates cousin had severe backache, incapacitated patient in teens. Associates to dream—feels arm become paralyzed when thinks of punching someone.

At times copes with anxiety by insulin injections.

Outraged at wife—had lump in his throat felt as big as a football.

On leaving for summer—discusses health with his doctor—no pressure on back of his head—general tone of health good. Much less fatigue.

Patient develops asthma-like attacks—following dreams of violence, dream of identification with father—when feeling of injustice and betrayal—are not effective in reducing achievement and success of house-venture.

Fatigue—during April—far less fatigue.

When in Europe—in charge of office—when opened morning mail—fear of anticipation of which might be in mail—always used to be followed by need to defecate—Reacts to demands negatively.

19. *How does intellectualization affect patient's life and work?*

Feels can't play competitive game in selling paintings—doesn't want people to buy his paintings on social basis.

Feels he has a moral obligation to the community—to paint as he does—for the viewer to understand his paintings.

Needs to win approval—takes on jobs doesn't want to—organized group of artists—then permitted himself to be pushed out. No desire to be known as an organizer but finds himself in this role.

20. *What about the obsessional defenses?*

With colleagues is passive, even subservient, until provoked extremely—then may have outburst, but following outburst again sees two sides to relationship.

Always must qualify positive steps in his work.

Dream—of a ritual—group of men walk through park to his house—perform ritual—urinate in room with urinals—while men and women officials watch. He comes in, has paper plastered to penis—doesn't urinate well, awkward—splatters wall —great embarrassment. (Obsession—must always negate own achievement—this time in relation to house.)

Patient always returns to obsessional thinking that only lack of time prevents him from painting more—time is his enemy —life is a race against time—has a dream of peaceful old age.

Feels his endless trivia which he finds himself repeating in his sessions is an injury to his pride—a need to experience treatment masochistically, therapist is doing this to him by not helping him to talk of more important things.

21. *Describe the effects of compulsive, rigid defenses.*

Always a rush to new activities—must make each new situation urgent—a demand of himself to get more out of each situation.

Can recall only one time when wanted to be some place joyously—walking home when shared apartment with fellow artist, a place of no censureship and no censorship.

Can only permit gratification when preoccupied; if not, censorship enters into activity.

22. *What about the sado-masochistic defenses?*

Used to feel despicable towards himself—thought he was subservient, avoided conflicts because wanted something for himself—opportunistic.

Same dream above—relates to wife and cousin—sado-masochistic defense "unless I take greater risks in what I'm doing, I can't reach higher goals."

Patient's sado-masochistic defense in its recurrent emphasis on injustice at demands of his wife has an obsessional quality. Patient says he has always detested the picture of the neurotic pitiful woman who preys upon her family with her invalidism —a weak heart—would hate to think of himself as this kind of person. In a way, thinks of his wife as this kind of person.

Has a fear of success—in painting moves away from perfecting a style.

May achieve some degree of perfection in one painting—but can't use this knowledge for the next painting—must start all over again (must separate result from continuum of process.) Flexibility in criticism of own painting—providing he qualifies this by feeling his awkwardness—painting goes from very good —then seems to fall apart—then may seem very good to him again.

23. *Describe the effects of repression and denial.*

Art school represented assertiveness—insisted upon going and to everyone's (family's) surprise succeeded. Art became a harbor for him—until this listless, a wanderer.

Denial becomes projection.

Patient says wife has ability to inject harm upon him with her deep sense of injustice by making him feel guilty.

Questionnaire #2: Submitted to therapist

(Period: October 1, 1958 - February 1, 1959)

PATIENT: MR. X

THERAPIST: DR. Y

1. *Give specific illustrations of the patient's self image.*

As father—some modifications of "good mother figure" to daughter in morning routine while wife sleeps. As teacher—

after intense quarrel with wife, is able to give lesson of high caliber to prominent people in publishing field. Has majority of women students, becomes less accepting of catering to them.

2. *What is the patient's behavior in relation to his wife like?*
Begins to see quarrels as mutually provocative pattern—less need to placate and patch things up.

3. *What is his behavior in relation to his colleagues?*
Feels it an injustice and envy on part of colleagues that he is not accepted into the Audubon Society.

4. *What is his relation to the therapist?*
In dreams initiates sex play with therapist, feels awkward. Dreams of being foetus position in dumbwaiter carried from basement of house to street level—through a series of a combination of aggressive and dependent incidents emerges into a new country with therapist waiting on the dock. In sessions thinks therapist is making demands on him to restrain anger with wife—confesses to this in mechanical way, followed by increase of asthma attacks.

5. *How does he react to exploitation or injustice by others?*
In the above sense, he feels exploited by therapist.

6. *How does he deal with his dependency needs (is illness used?)*
This combined with alternate pattern of many weeks of hostility in dreams and towards wife leads to increase in asthma attacks. Patient finally brings breathing attacks into sessions to gratify dependency needs and to feel accepted.

7. *What are the artist's relationships to professional colleagues?*
Competes with colleagues to be admitted to special group (Academy of Sciences). Is furious and feels it an injustice not to be accepted. Continues painting but during this period begins to make large drawings with some vague plan that he will have a show of drawings.

8. *What expectations does the artist have of his work?*
Expectations of his work subside as patient gains awareness of patterns. "The fear of destroying all the good that exists though he knows he can do better—leave good enough alone on the basis of compromise rather than acceptance"—How repetition of subject matter takes over to destroy gratifications and judgment.

9. *What are his attitudes toward exhibition or sale of his paintings?*

Has several exhibits in East Hampton, L.I. This community has symbolically become a place of refuge for him. Is accepted, feels no demands are made upon him, sells paintings here as a steady market, etc. Does manage to sell individual paintings steadily in New York too, and asks high prices: $600, $800, and up.

10. *Tell some of the patient's dreams in this period.*

Dreams of collector H.W. who exchanges objets d'art with him but who has never, in reality, bought his paintings. Dreams of competitions with members of family—wife, daughter, cousin—always on unjust criticism and he is helpless before expressing rage or after.

11. *Tell some of the patient's fantasies.*

Can defend anyone else's causes but his own. Sees a TV film of nun, Sister Acquinas, a non-conformist who leads some progressive cause—identifies with her. He too will be a non-conformist—will not compromise political values to achieve social and artistic recognition.

Sees another TV film of *The Sea Wolf*—the old ruined ex-doctor climbs to top of mast, jeered at by the sailors, finally screams back curse of defiance before hurling himself into the sea. Patient has asthmatic attack. He too is old and ruined, victim of injustice—his anger gets him nowhere. There is no way out.

12. *Give specific examples of the expression of hostility toward cousin and mother.*

In associating to the limits that cousin seems to have imposed upon him, patient recalls memories of scattered expressions of hostility—one memory gives patient violent backache during session (similar backache around same incident last June). This incident is where cousin, through accident or rheumatic condition, is unable to walk. Patient now thinks of not visiting cousin as hostility towards him. Mother's and wife's complaints are that he doesn't pay enough attention to their needs. Patient begins to wonder if his non-giving is an expression of hostility.

Patient brings in a dream mother has. (First time mother has told him her dreams.) In dream, he has borrowed mother's car, but it is out of control. He may kill someone. She calls police. Following this dream there is a break-through of hostility in dreams sustained over a two-month period.

13. *Give illustrations of masochistic behavior and feeling.*
Focus with wife—in numerous incidents.

14. *How does hostility show in his art?*
Following expressions of rage towards wife, patient is able to complete painting he worked on since the summer. These expressions of rage are experienced as assertiveness and hostility in contrast to former expressions of rage which left him helpless and frustrated since the need for acceptance would lead to conforming and compromise.

15. *Does hostility appear in fantasy?*
Recalls with a feeling of shame an incident when he was 18, when he made a grandiose statement to cousin's friends that he would be famous some day. Still the need to prove this to his cousin.

16. *Does hostility appear in dreams?*
Two-month period of dreams expressing hostility. Patient indicates the anal character of his dreams. Many dreams of back alleys, passageways. In one dream, a dummy on the back seat of a car, pulling out the back way from a garage, is bouncing up and down. If it was a real person, his skull would be crushed. Patient associates to his third-grade teacher who humiliated him, forced him into position of a dummy and crushed his spirit. Patient dreams he must be deformed like a dwarf to accomplish things. There are confused dreams of men fighting each other with knives and violence while other men who seem to be the same men are floundering in the water. There is a dream of becoming a member of a non-conformist organization where he is chosen to poison someone —at the showdown, patient exclaims that if non-conforming means to kill, he must give it up. There is a dream of himself as a gorilla but a friendly one who steals marble (sculpture) transformed into a germ culture (illness—guilt), but who is very gentle in his care of two children.

17. *Does hostility affect sexual relationships?*
Beginning change in sexual relationships. Patient needed sex compulsively to reassure self of acceptance—wife felt sex as a demand made upon her and so as a hostility. Patient more

directly assertive of his need for mutual acceptance. Sex less frequent.

18. *Please describe psychosomatic ailments (fatigue, asthma, hay fever, others.)*

Only one major symptom during this period—breathing attacks becoming asthmatic. Depression and fatigue occur rarely, are absorbed within the asthma.

At first, asthma occurs directly as need for attention. Patient expressed this quite directly. He has always been the responsible, independent figure with colleagues, . . . as teacher, and as head of the household (not in terms of respect for status but demands upon him). With diabetes, he took his daily shots of insulin and was as healthy as anyone. Asthma is different. It makes one an invalid. One cannot rush oneself. One must conserve one's energy for important matters (his painting). At first patient's breathing attacks seem to him to be ignored by family. As they become more severe and he is under medical care for it, some attention is paid to him but he feels it quickly denied to him as his wife begins to feel sicker and sicker with one complaint after another. Despite his asthma, he is again in position of taking over household chores, etc.

During the period that hostility increases, asthma increases in severity to balance and negate the hostility, and to assure for himself some measure of acceptance on the basis of illness. (Patient says he hates the image of the neurotic woman with the heart condition who keeps the entire family enslaved—in referring to his asthma.)

Behind the screen of the asthma, patient works through so much hostility—brings it to a head in the sessions—therapist becomes a mother transference figure and patient works through a period at age 18. He was working as a waiter to earn enough money to go to Europe to study art. He developed a hernia. Had an incompetent operation, hemorrhaged, one of his testicles collapsed and began to atrophy. He was very weak. Developed hay fever and then finally, when he had what he feels was a nervous breakdown with hay fever—his mother came to the rescue. In reaction to the fear of his expression of hostility (reverse castration above)—patient had several asthmatic attacks in sessions, with the asthma then beginning to subside.

19. What about the obsessional defenses?
Obsessions and rigidity are also experienced as hostility to repetition.

20. What about the sado-masochistic defenses?
The sado-masochistic defense of *being caught* and the injustice of the situations—particularly as it was repeated in countless incidents with his wife—gives way to the sadism—a more direct expression of hostility. The masochism—the asthma, to gain acceptance. Patient gradually displaces the sado-masochism and feels he is not caught by *them*, wife, mother, artists, etc. Following the recall of a memory of mother calling his father obscene names, patient experienced intense affect, breathing attack in session—experienced his own helplessness as similar to his father and along with a shift of defenses began to experience a fear and need of relations with men—much material about friend who died when patient was 27, right after his marriage to wife—Dream about daughter's sexual relationship to patient.

21. Describe workings of repression and denial.
Used repression—denial and intellectualization abundantly.

The following chapters present a double approach:
    I—Clinical studies of the history, psycho-
    dynamics and unfolding therapy
    II—Various other measurements and conden-
    sations of the relationship between
    psychodynamics and work habits in each
    patient
For the most part the clinical sections were prepared by the respective therapist-collaborators. The research sections were prepared by Dr. Fried. In order to protect the identity of the patients we have omitted linking the name of each author with the clinical section. We are indebted to the American Journal of Orthopsychiatry for releasing much of the clinical material used in one case history. The material was somewhat changed and edited for use in one of the clinical sections. However, specific credit is due to each of the therapists for the preparation of data from which the clinical presentations were prepared, in some cases by the therapists and in other cases by the chief author.

CHAPTER 3

The Case of Matthew Taylor, a Sculptor

Case Report

M ATTHEW TAYLOR IS A well-known sculptor who was forty-five
years old when he entered treatment. He had been married for
over twenty years to an attractive, imaginative, lively and demanding woman, a dancer, on whom he was extremely dependent. The marriage was stormy and often came close to the breaking point. The couple's only child, a boy, had died soon after
birth and neither parent seemed to miss, at least consciously,
the experience of raising a family.

Matthew, at the time of starting therapy, worked as a curator
of a large museum. The terms of his job allowed him equal time
for work at the museum and his own creative work. Matthew
came to treatment because of prolonged and severe personality
difficulties. These showed up primarily in his marriage but were
equally damaging in his relations with art dealers, collectors,
colleagues and in teaching positions he had held. He had lost
many sources of livelihood because of quarrels.

Matthew Taylor had an infantile character with strong oral
fixations. There existed a permeating, mild, chronic depression,
occasionally intensified to a level of severe depressive episodes.
He had made one serious suicidal attempt. Other symptomatic
manifestations were compulsive and intellectualizing defenses,
which hampered the artist's creative efforts since he felt hemmed
in and unfree. When this sense of being "tight" was pronounced
the depressive tendencies were intensified. The artist felt that
he was worthless because he was not working well. There was
a strong tendency toward passive dependent relationships, especially with his wife and males in authority positions. Accom-

panying the passive dependent strivings were pronounced defenses against them by rages and attempts to abandon the individual on whom dependency focused.

Matthew's parents were well-to-do French people who settled in America when the child was seven. His early youth was
spent in Western Europe, particularly in Paris where the parents, who were in their middle years when their only son was
born, led an active social life. The boy was brought up in an
authoritarian fashion. He was exposed to many Spartan restrictions, such as never being permitted to wash himself in the
morning with anything but ice cold water, having only a meager
allowance which left no room for self-indulgence, and being
asked, even as a small boy, to perform many chores around the
home, even though the family had servants. The avowed purpose of such demands was sensible enough: the boy should learn
early to cope with the stringencies of life. However, the manner
in which these often taxing requests were enforced was quite
harsh and flowed out of the parents' unconscious sadistic tendencies.

At the same time the parents worshiped their son, whom they
considered in the genius caliber and of whom they had the
highest expectations. He was to become a great artist, an outstanding scientist, or a leading politician. Undoubtedly he was
expected to fulfill the parents' narcissistic ambitious expectations, which they felt they themselves had only approached.

There was constant quarreling in the family, and he witnessed
many violent verbal battles between mother and father, and
father and uncle. He was frequently drawn into these as a cats-
paw.

We are beginning to see that Matthew was exposed in his
childhood to a bewildering series of pressures. At the same time
that excessive Spartan restrictions were placed on him, he was
pampered and over-indulged and his precocity, particularly in
intellectual matters, was stimulated, lauded and paraded before
relatives and friends. Deprived of small physical comforts on
the one hand and excessively applauded on the other, there did
not appear to have been a warm attachment to the mother or
any other figure at the level of a *child*. He felt solitary and exploited.

Matthew learned to defend himself against feelings of loneliness and helplessness by using his intellect. He was encouraged by some members of his family to make verbal attacks upon his father, which went unreprimanded. He still tends to make contact with people through provocation and intellectual brilliance rather than through direct affective channels. Thus while he has enormous longings for close relationships, these are thwarted by his inability to realize the extent to which he can alienate people by attacks of verbal cruelty. His inability to sense the effect of his tirades stems from the denial and repression of the reality of his feelings in his early years when rages and tantrums were directed toward his family. By the time he entered treatment he still expected to be allowed to get away with such ranting, as though he were still a bright but badly behaved child. This had gotten him into all sorts of difficulty in his professional and home life. Not recognizing the degree of his hostility, he was surprised at the retaliations of colleagues and his wife. This in turn threatened his great need for security and tended to provoke a circular pattern of intellectualizing, withdrawal, defensive hostility, rigidity and blocking of creativity.

In early childhood Matthew had difficulty in making warm affective contact with his mother. He felt that she was "immutably unreasonable" and this generated an overwhelming hostility in him. To counteract the frustration of his dependent needs he developed in his early years a fascination with female body-like shapes, which carried over into preoccupation with maternal anatomical forms in his work.

Simultaneously frustrations were accompanied by rages within him which he experienced and continued to experience as a threat to the loved and needed person. He feared that he would either destroy or be destroyed by the maternal figure. He appeared to be caught between this fear of destruction and the need for direct reassurance at an almost infantile level, centering around oral activities. Being fearful of his own impulses and their destructive propensities, he tended to rely upon intellectualizing defenses, both in general thinking and creative work. Under the impact of such intellectualizing defensiveness he was inclined to "stay put," to "close up," to become artistically rigid. He tended to cling to given models of style, and as he grew older to avoid the spontaneous expression of his own inner creativity. He could allow himself freedom only when the way was shown by someone else.

In the five years preceding treatment Matthew had become considerably freer in his artistic work, and attributed much of the freedom to the example of his wife. She had learned to be completely free in her dancing and took the lead in drawing him into her world of creation and artistic expression. He felt reassurance and an immense increase in his own spontaneity. Even toward the close of therapy he could allow himself to be spontaneously creative mainly when he made sketches for a work. In such preliminary activity he has found great spontaneity. Once the sketch is completed he tends to become stereotyped and formal, too conventional and intellectual.

In periods when Matthew's relationship with his wife or some other female figure was going well, that is, when he felt loved and when rage and compulsive intellectual controls of rage were not needed, he could be spontaneous and creative. When he was rejected in any way by a woman, he tended to become sterile, tight, conventional and generally withdrawn and depressed.

Infantile rage and its projection onto the maternal figure, operating at an unconscious level, had the effect of making the patient feel impotent and unmanly, and of raising to dangerous proportions passive homosexual tendencies and fears of these tendencies. During childhood Matthew had developed no enduring identification with a man. His father was conceived of as a weak, foolish individual, dominated by females in the household. This posed a double problem: 1) He could not, by identifying himself with a strong father, master his fears of women because the man who should have lent him strength was himself ineffectual with women; his helpless rage at women was therefore intensified. 2) His attacks upon his father and his childhood fears that these might materialize in the form of destruction of the father were underscored because neither father nor any other family member had successfully stopped the boy's tantrum. Thus he continued to be fearful of his omnipotence. The dynamic tendencies toward his father were illustrated in dreams. In one, his father was serving him a dish. This was a reference to cunnilingus, as if the father, too, was unable to function in a potent heterosexual masculine role. (Matthew had occasional bouts of severe potency difficulties.) Other dreams dealt with his father being dead, accompanied by undertones that the patient was responsible. In one dream Matthew was wearing the uniform of a general, but realized that he was only in costume.

Matthew tended to isolate himself from mature competition. His attitude toward money and economic realities was that of a leisured gentleman. Being unrealistic, this carried with it a pre-cariousness with regard to jobs, material security, etc., intensi-fying Matthew's dependent position. His parents, in his fourth year, seized on an illness which later cleared up completely, to encourage him to remain dependent upon his family. He was often told to avoid real competition and encouraged to pamper himself physically. All through childhood he was terribly fearful of direct physical aggression. He never had an opportunity to test his strength or to develop ego strength in dealing with sim-ple, material details of living. He had never made a living until he was thirty-eight. He never owned a house or wrestled with monetary details of everyday living, but preserved the illusion of the favored child. This fostered the narcissistic, dependent and omnipotent strivings described above.

Matthew's faulty masculine identification made him more de-pendent upon women's approval and more compulsively in need of reassurance about his potency (through adequate sexual per-formance) to bolster him against castration anxiety. This added another emphasis to his oral dependent fixation and to the some-what deficient grasp of reality in regard to his instinctual strivings.

A dynamic pattern, related to his creativity, followed from the above. The patient was confused about his own considerable facility with forms. He was fearful and distrustful of the need (in his artistic work) for realism. He was ambivalent about his capacity for skillful use of real form. Being vaguely aware of his deficient reality grasp in relation to control of his instinctual strivings and to the acute problems of living, he had a greater need for externally-imposed forms in art. This made for conflict. He was aware of a tendency toward derivativeness in his sculpture, which he had to fight because it had the connotation of passive submission and was experienced as an attempt to identify himself passively with a stronger artist. Although he realized intellectually that all art is derivative, he found himself unable to use his fine sense of form to its fullest extent or to abandon its use temporarily because of the defensive function it served.

There were a number of dynamic tendencies not directly related to creativity, which could be expected to increase his creativity eventually in a collateral way. For example, the relationship with his wife occupied a central position in his economy. He had married a woman who personified some of his fantasies about the nature of women; she was given to extraordinary hostile outbursts and was herself a confused and unreasonable person. Because of the nature of the fantasies he had entertained about women all his life, he was not aware that she was deviant in this regard until quite late in their relationship. He was totally unequipped to handle her outbursts in a realistic way. He had remained tied to her over the years by one or another mechanism, the chief of which was the projection that his wife would go to pieces if he left her. There was some reality to this, but it also represented his own feeling of helplessness. The one suicide attempt he made occurred when he felt that *she* was leaving *him*. It was felt that when he could be helped to gain a more mature, independent status in place of the infantile dependency upon his wife, and that when they could achieve a more mature, heterosexual level, instead of the "two babes in the woods" regressive relationship, many of the infantile fears that contaminated his relation to his creative work could be expected to diminish. Thus the analysis of any part of his neurosis was expected to increase his integrative capacity, and indirectly, his creativity.

On the negative side, there were signs that his creative work had some narcissistic, exhibitionistic, status-and-power motivations which were reactions against a dependent position. It was possible that as the need for such defensive uses of work decreased, his total energy output might be somewhat reduced. He had strong needs to be first in everything he did and could not tolerate competition. Although neurotic, this had the effect of spurring the mechanical output of work. How much a reduction in anxiety would reduce the quantity of his work could not be predicted at the outset. It was also possible that he might turn from the currently fashionable in art toward a more traditional style, which might not meet with critical acceptance but which might better serve his own needs.

One element of Matthew's pathology was his need to make women feel inferior and subordinate. This has not previously been stressed, but it was discernable from the patient's material and was a frequent complaint of his wife. This appeared to be a reaction formation. In a few of his works there was a tendency to depreciate women. One statue of a female figure is entitled something equivalent to "Mother Whore."

Matthew showed ambivalence about style. Artistic tendencies alternated between realism and formalism on the one hand, and abstract free expression on the other. He was inclined to oppose whatever tendency was in the foreground, in a stubborn, negativistic way.

Predictions

Prediction #1

As the patient becomes more aware of the pathological nature of his verbal intellectualizing and of the use of provocation and attack as a defense against helplessness, he will lean less on these defenses. As a result: 1) *he will have greater security with his wife and colleagues. He will be less given to intellectualizing, less defensively provocative, and more trusting of his real creative talents.* 2) *As, in particular, the intellectualizing defenses will be gradually abandoned, the present periods of rigidity and compulsive symmetry in his work may dissolve.*

Results: *Both these predictions came true.*

Prediction #2

The patient will become more aware of the infantile nature

of his rage toward a frustrating woman. He will become aware of and give up omnipotent thoughts. He will more readily recognize his tendency to project this violent rage onto the woman, will become increasingly capable of dealing realistically with frustrations, of maintaining female contacts, and of resolving the realistic problems that may exist. As a result: 1) *he will be able to distinguish more clearly between spontaneous creative effort and reactive infantile impulses of destructive violence.* 2) *The grandiosity that now interferes with his work will decline.* 3) *Insofar as he can resolve problems with his wife, she can give him more security and he will be less apt to suffer real frustrations in his emotional and sexual life, thus freeing more energy for creative work.*

Results: *All three predictions came true.*

Prediction #3

The transference affords the patient an opportunity for a new identification with a male. Repeated working through of his quarrels with women, with the analyst's support for a realistic stand toward unreasonable demands, will help him to deal with his wife's anger or unreasonableness in a more mature way. Working through of the negative side of the transference and his hostility toward the analyst on numerous occasions will help him feel less endangered by what he fantasies to be the destructive propensities of his hostile feelings. The therapeutic task is a dual one: since the hostility is largely unconscious, he tends to be sharply critical without being aware of it; at the same time he is fearful of the strength of his hostility. By helping him to recognize when he is hostile and by meeting it squarely, some reduction of tension in this area is to be expected. This should be recognizable in more realistic feelings toward male colleagues and toward women. As he feels less impotent, there should be more freedom in creativity. A lessened need for internal controls should result in a much looser approach to creative work.

Results: *This prediction came true.*

Prediction #4

A calculated exploration of analytic technique is contemplated with this patient. Though such attempts have just been begun in the analysis, a rather free discussion is being allowed between patient and analyst of the material details of living. Working through of the material arrangements for treatment, finances, etc., will afford him an opportunity to increase the realism with which he views his relationships with the world; in effect, to increase his ego strength. As he becomes better able to deal with the material world it is expected that feelings of impotence, helplessness and dependency will be modified, which will in turn reduce his anxieties surrounding these needs. *This will free him of some of his dependency upon external forms, with a greater trust in his own resources and creativity.* (The patient has a tendency to entertain ideas that he is either much brighter, wiser, and more sophisticated than the analyst or that he is helplessly ignorant, compared to the analyst, of the nature of the material world. Through the medium of free discussion of the details of everyday living, with appropriate interpretation of these two opposing tendencies, some gain in ego strength is expected.)

Results: *The prediction came true.*

Prediction #5

When the patient rids his creative work of compulsive derivativeness and externally-imposed forms, as protection against anxiety about instinctual strivings, *he will become less restrained. Also, when he learns to distinguish between free use of his own facility and passive submission and dependency on a stronger artist, he will be free to be traditional or visual or realistic if he happens to choose to do so, without anxiety. This tendency can already be detected in the patient's recent work.*

Results: *This prediction came true.*

Prediction #6

It seems apparent that the need to depreciate women can be modified in various ways, stemming as it does from a reaction against passive helplessness and dependency. One would expect to see in his work the emergence of less ambivalent relations to female figures. Artistically, this may not be important.

Results: *The prediction came true and influenced creative patterns in the sense that preoccupation with women and marriage diminished and more energy was freed for creative work.*

Directions of Development and Ratings*

Dynamics

1. Passivity (dependency) — defensive quarreling and provocations —true assertion   (6)

2. Intellectualization (as defense) —affective explosions—acting out —affective involvement with wife and others   (6.5)
3. Defensive hostility, often not recognized, towards women and colleagues—sexual acting out— recognizing hostility—companionable relations   (6)
4. Lack of masculine identification —testing in transference—hostility toward males—masculine identification   (6.5)
5. Planless living and anxiety about it—spurts of planning—self-pity —planful living   (6.5)
6. Ambivalence towards the female —intense criticisms of female— distinction between real and fantasied aspects of specific females—appreciation of specific female   (7.5)
7. Contacts through intellectual brilliance — through affective channels   (6)

8. Compulsiveness — quarrelsome, anxiety — more mature affective expression   (5)
9. Overestimation of omnipotence and own aggression — anxious — realistic evaluation of aggression   (6.5)
10. Low frustration tolerance — sexual adventures when frustrated — tolerant of frustration   (5)

Work Patterns

I. High degree of ego and superego control and lack of inner freedom — loosening of controls and freedom   (6)
II. Neurotic drain of energy felt as lethargy — higher spirits   (8)

III. Depressions interfering with work — medication and relief — approaching work joyously, still with medication   (6)

IV. Compulsive geometrical symmetry — freedom from such symmetry   (8)

V. Deplores mixture of "safe" and "bold" stroke — achieves pure style   (6)
VI. Inhibited from v i s u a l i z i n g readily — visualizing clearly and at will   (8)

VII. Guilt over use of doodles and other external stimulants of creativity — guiltless acceptance of many stimulants   (7)
VIII. Compelled to deviate from and discard sketches — utilizes sketches and models   (8)
IX. Compelled to create masterworks and destroys work — disregards acclaim enough to create independently   (7)

*The ratings reflect forward movement made by the patient within the various areas as measured along a nine-point scale. A rating of one would signify no movement, a rating of five signifies that a mid-point has been reached, and nine that the patient has moved so far as to have achieved complete success. Note that the ratings in the dynamics column are based on the answers furnished by the therapist, and the ratings in the work pattern column are based on data furnished by the artist patient.

The ratings themselves were made by two researcher-judges, and each rating reflects the mean of the two judges' ratings.

Discussion of Size and Distribution of Ratings

The ratings we have presented, which are based on the last evaluation made, reflect the state of affairs after roughly three years of treatment. They show that treatment progressed, one might say, better than satisfactorily. Only one direction of development—that from compulsiveness to an openly and freely integrated affective life—shows a mid-point rating of five. Considering the fact that compulsive defenses and character traits are particularly slow in giving way to other modalities of regulation, that is indeed to be taken as a sign that treatment "took" and that Matthew was well along the road to change.

The changes are all-embracing, for as we see, no direction of development, that is, no significant area of functioning, has remained static. Everywhere there is change, with no backward movement. This is of particular interest as far as the development of work patterns is concerned. We would generally assume that a person undergoing treatment changes favorably as far as his personality, that is, the dynamic forces that determine his life, are concerned. But remember, our initial and most accentuated hypothesis was that we need not be disturbed to be creatively active; that pathology is not a prerequisite for creativity. This was the hypothesis to be disproved, or supported. In this case, not one of the work attitudes making up the frame of mind that determines the artist's ability to engage himself vitally in work, was found to have deteriorated as a result of psychoanalytic therapy. On the contrary, as far as the mental activities with which he undertakes his work are concerned, all show marked improvement. *He was aided to approach his work with much better mental-emotional-visual, attitudes.*

It is particularly interesting to note that the development along direction of development IV under work patterns (compulsive geometric symmetry—freedom from such symmetry) is given a rating of eight. By contrast, the corresponding direction of development in dynamics #8 (compulsiveness—more mature affective expression) is only rated five. In other words, there is more development within the creative work area than can be noted as characterizing the total functioning of the personality. This may result from the different ways in which the artist and the therapist assessed the two situations. In view of the tendency of this patient to be pessimistic, depressed, even morose, this appears unlikely. For all in all, he views progress generally with several grains of salt. Rather, it seems that he "leads" in the work area, that the gradually evolving changes affected the work area first.

The changes in dynamics in general, while not as pronounced as the changes in the work area, are uniform and on a good level.

All changes in the two areas, dynamics and work patterns, appear intimately related. For instance, the artist overestimates his omnipotence and aggression a good deal less at this point in treatment than at the beginning, as the rating of 6:5 in direction of development #9 (dynamics) indicates. Surely this development is correlated with that along direction IX (work patterns) showing that he is no longer as compelled to create omnipotent masterworks and thus less likely to destroy works that are found to be—often temporarily—less than eminent.

As stated elsewhere, all changes that took place, both in dynamics and in the work pattern area, were predicted at the nine months' point in treatment. However, one prediction, namely that the depressions would clear up, did not materialize, although they were less acute and less chronic. No totally unexpected change in the creative area occurred.

Changes of Work Patterns

At the beginning of treatment Matthew alternated between productive and unproductive periods. Like the other artists in this project, he came to psychoanalytic therapy not because of working difficulties—although these existed and pained him —but for other reasons, already outlined. As the table shows, the patient's work patterns were improved along various dimensions.

He suffered from periodic work blocks. He described the condition of being blocked as being in a fog, being constipated, tight, wishing to fiddle away time without "reaching a pitch," or as being bogged down in ritual. He felt at such times that he was too concerned with the logical, and this made him listless. When he started treatment he had already acquired inner means of getting through such a blocked condition, and so was not hopelessly stuck in the blocked state. During treatment he described the leading up to the creative phase as unpleasant. However, the transition once made, creative "jumps" occurred which had little to do with reason and which felt pleasant. The subjective experience of "unpleasure" on the road from blocked condition to "being stirred" was a deterrent from moving out of the blocked condition. At the end of treatment less "unpleasure" was connected with this transition.

In this case the blocked condition was the result of excessive ego and superego controls that Matthew had developed as defense against strong and violent instinctive urges. In particular, oral desires of devouring and incorporating, and anal wishes to release explosively played a role. In the course of inhibiting these urges, a rather universal condition of self-inhibition, rigidity, and affective block resulted. The patient himself stated repeatedly that he felt "in his guts" that art is close to primitive biological tendencies and that reason is not the primary mainspring.

His history abounds with incidents illustrating the presence of intense rage impulses. He had once slashed his wrists and continued to feel a periodic desire to slash them; he would have liked to go hunting but was afraid of carrying a gun for fear of the impulse to misuse it. He often had dreams of whipping someone to death, and in his daily life also had the wish to beat and hit. As previously stated, Matthew's wife is an impulsive woman, expressing her emotions and impulses very freely, and by identifying with her he could, in a roundabout way, obtain emotional discharge from time to time. He said that since she had begun to function "as an extension of myself, I function better in my art."

During periods of excessive control—such periods might extend from one day to several months—fine, gentle strokes and a preoccupation with detail replaced strong, bold movements in his sculptures. Toward the end of treatment he noted that parallel with a growing freedom from the constricted, blocked condition, boldness of conception and stroke prevailed. The degree of emancipation from the controlled condition is reflected in the rating six.

On entering treatment Matthew felt chronically lethargic and depressed, and in such moods contemplated work with reluctance. The lethargy was perceived by the therapist as another result of the vast amounts of energy that had to be inhibited due to the primitive oral nature of the drives and to the great amount of aggression. When the patient became familiar with the nature of the inhibited energy and could afford to loosen controls, the lethargy lifted. This is illustrated by the high rating of eight.

In the beginning of treatment Matthew was compelled towards geometrical symmetry in his works. Such symmetry was not the result of free choice or of connections between symmetry and beauty, or symmetry and the artist's image. Rather the symmetry was a "must" and gave to the fine creations repetitiveness and restriction. The presence of symmetry lessened his anxiety, and its absence intensified anxiety. Thus by "hook or crook" he had to establish symmetry. As treatment progressed, the compulsion to introduce geometrical symmetry dissolved until at the end of treatment he stated in the questionnaire: "I am now free of the compulsions and inhibitions to use geometrical symmetry." The patient connected the symmetry of his sculptures in some measure with the fine symmetrical shape of his own body. By contrast he ascribed his wife's greater artistic freedom to some extent to her less symmetrical body.

The need for symmetry in the early phases of treatment was dynamically connected with a system of obsessive-compulsive doubts and a compulsion to balance impulses with controls. Matthew remarked that he desired to be both antagonist and protagonist of any idea he entertained. He would first expound an idea, then run it down in his mind, ending with a nihilistic sense of defeat. When the hairline balance between drive and control, between antagonist and protagonist, gradually gave way, with the impulses occasionally in the fore; when, in other words, the psyche itself was not so sharply divided into two factions, the preoccupation with symmetry ceased.

Another fluctuation which often led to minute-by-minute changes was between enthusiasm and pessimism about work. This flux was the basis of considerable anxiety and created a reluctance to work. When he was in the throes of enthusiasm, he would begin to anticipate the low ebb and the reduction in output that accompanied it. This ebb and flow was related to changes in the ego-superego balance. When ego and superego controls were tight, gloom prevailed; when controls, as well as guilt, were lower, optimism ruled. These mood changes were considerably reduced at the end of treatment, with a steadier level of optimism in the foreground, as the rating of six shows.

At the beginning of treatment Matthew's sculptures consisted primarily of animal figures. Towards the middle of treatment he began to fluctuate between human and animal figures. This fluctuation reminded him of the way he got an erection in intercourse, then lost it. To observers of his dynamics the fluctuations between human and animal figures seemed connected with his fluctuations between impulse freedom and impulse control, between elation and guilt. Drawing the human figure was here connected with guilt about sexual impulses. Early in puberty he had drawn nude female figures to excite himself. The expectation of punishment—both by external figures and his own superego—led him to abstain from such drawings as soon as he could gratify sexual urges in other ways, however inadequate.

The sculptor used to wake in the morning with severe headaches and depressions, the latter often lasting through the day. The depressions were caused by a multiplicity of factors, among them his dissatisfaction with assuming an adult male role. Medication was prescribed in order to enable him to work. While the depressions became less intense and occurred periodically rather than daily, by the time the last questionnaire was administered the patient was still dependent on medication. We rated this development six.

Before coming to treatment Matthew took dexedrine and dexamyl to help him emerge from the blocked state, to get hold of the inner stimulation and approach a free condition. The dexedrine helped him obtain a state of elation. At the end of treatment he still took a dexedrine type of stimulant—he shifted to Daprisal combined with Cafergot—to serve the same purpose. The dosage of the stimulant had decreased; tablets were taken sometimes only twice a week instead of five to seven times as they had been previously. Both patient and therapist did not consider the intake of the medicine a particularly notable symptom but were more concerned with the freezing of emotion that made discharge of anger and other impulses difficult and often led to headaches necessitating use of stimulants.

The patient admired Picasso and what he called the Dionysian school of painters—Renaissance painters particularly—who were not blocked, or as he usually put it, "not constipated." He occasionally was able to free himself from his inner constriction by contemplating Picassos and the work of other free artists.

Matthew could "start himself" working in these artificial ways when he entered treatment. During treatment he acquired greater inner fluidity which helped him make the transition from a controlled state of mind (strong ego and superego control) to a condition of inner freedom (ego reduction, ego regression). Medication continued to contribute to the transition. In addition he used another method, about which he had felt guilty in the beginning of treatment. Doodling, or handling and contemplating accidentally-assembled objects (objects trouvés) got him into a creative, alert, stimulated condition. But he felt guilty about having recourse to such devices. "There is in me a pressure that the work spring out of the forehead of Zeus. This is one of the retarding things in modern art, a phobia of being derivative, the necessity to deny the parenthood of the work." Toward the end of treatment, he was less intolerant of divergent sources of inspiration. If the fusion of two pieces of material excited him, it was all right. If doodling, or contemplating a Picasso or Noguchi sent him into visual fervor, he was satisfied to accept this as a valid motivation to work, as direction VII indicates.

At the beginning of treatment the artist had difficulty following sketches. Ideas for these came effortlessly, and were free of tightness, intellectuality and self-doubt. They were splendid work models, according to the artist's own conviction. Yet he felt compelled to abandon them. He stated: "Unfortunately I rarely let myself rely on my sketches. With most artists of post-Renaissance Western culture I share the inclination, I might even say compulsion, to deviate from the sketch. So I hope finally to learn to rely on my sketches. I revert to too much control without my sketches. Changes made are rarely an improvement." During treatment the artist did develop a much more accepting attitude toward his sketches and worked increasingly with them. Thus at the end of treatment he said in the questionnaire: "I have finally learned to stay with the essential form concept of a sketch. I am not compelled any longer to deviate from the initial style. There will be minor changes and evolvements but no changes of the form character."

Megalomanic aspirations stood in the way of productivity early in treatment. Matthew used art, in his own words, to get himself "on a pedestal to be admired by the world." He wanted each piece to be a masterwork, or, as he put it, "to be the greatest statement ever." These aspirations led him to destroy many supposedly mediocre works which in retrospect he evaluated as fine pieces of art. Also these aspirations deterred him from starting work, since he expected to fall short of the impossibly high level he set himself. This condition changed considerably. The artist became more preoccupied with the product than with the evaluation of it. Moreover, as his level of creativity and expertness moved out of the fantasy realm and became an experienced reality, he was much more satisfied with his work. Thus he stated in the last questionnaire that he now usually liked the pieces he completed and knew that others liked them too. In the first questionnaire, by contrast, he had set forth conflicting attitudes about reception of his work. He professed indifference to the evaluation of his work by others, yet became irritated with "ignorant" critics. Both the professed indifference and the irritation in fact represented different ways of dealing with extraordinary, unsatisfied, ambitions.

CHAPTER 4

The Case of Jonathan Norton, a Painter

Case Report

Jonathan Norton is an attractive, sturdy, well-built man in his early forties. The diagnosis was of a passive-aggressive psychoneurotic personality with obsessional sado-masochistic defensive structure and several chronic psychosomatic conditions.

The patient was a recognized painter on a high, though not outstanding, level. He had had several one-man shows and still retained an inactive affiliation with a good art gallery that sponsored him. He was dissatisfied and discouraged by a lack of productivity for several years, and by the declining quality of his work. He related this change to constant quarreling with his wife and to extreme fatigue, and had doubts about his talent.

He felt that he had reached the peak of his painting during the pre-war period of the 1930's. At that time his representational paintings of social protest were well received in the art world, and much was predicted for his potential as an artist. Since then there had been an increasing struggle to find a style of his own, with little self-gratification at the results. Newspaper and magazine art reviews harped on his potential. His paintings had been judged on a par with contemporary artists who had since left him far behind. He was disturbed at the reaction of fellow artists who accepted him socially but not professionally. These inner problems were acted out in bitter sado-masochistic involvement with his wife, with recurring themes of betrayal and injustice. In his paintings at this time he was preoccupied with rabbis and patriarchal figures, which were poorly realized.

[57]

Frustration with his painting contributed to his masochistic needs.

Guilt and fear were hidden beneath the daily quarrels. Jonathan linked these feelings to his cousin and talked about them in a self-pitying, confessional manner, with no insight into how this contributed to inhibition in his creativity. He said that his cousin, not he, should have been the painter in the family. In his opinion, his cousin's talent was of genius caliber, fluid and intuitive.

Projection, denial, and isolation were other defenses affecting creativity and maintaining repression of inner conflicts. His warm, outgoing personality was used to disarm and please, and made for a detached, spurious feeling of self in his relating to family, friends and painting.

The patient's cousin, twelve years older and living in the patient's parental home for many years, had introduced him to painting and then himself had given it up. He was now a successful advertising man. At fourteen, Jonathan had taken his cousin's painting, and presenting it as his own had won a city-wide contest. He remembered with embarrassment and humiliation the ridicule of his cousin and others when he said he would be a famous artist some day. Despite later confirmation of his own talent he persisted in the idea that his cousin, not he, should have been the artist. He lived in vague dread that his cousin would return to painting and outdistance him. This fear was constantly re-enacted with fellow artists, with guilt projected as betrayal and injustice.

His father, who died when Jonathan was twenty-two, had been a shadowy figure dominated and humiliated by his wife, and living for the most part in the quiet circle of his music, unrelated to the family. In the last few days of his life he had encouraged his son to become an artist. His mother reprimanded Jonathan for not being at his father's bedside when he died, and the "injustice" of her remark remained contrasted with his father's encouragement.

The patient felt that he, like his father, was just a shadow in the house. His cousin was openly preferred and favored. His mother told him that she had tried to abort him. She had felt no need for a child to interfere with her active community life. He recounted this in his usual self-pitying way. Despite this constant detailing of injustices, he was aware of no hostility in himself, but saw himself as patriarchal, humorous and philosophical. Injustice was his fate in life. There was nothing he could do about it. These feelings were cover-all descriptions of his childhood, and he could report few actual memories. He did recall, however, that his cousin said of him that he walked around as though the world were an onion, always crying. Jonathan could not remember this about himself, but did think he had been lonely and poignantly recalled that at art school, where he became aware that he had talent, he felt he was like a boat entering a harbor of refuge. Art was his refuge.

Upon graduation he looked forward eagerly to a year abroad, which he expected his cousin to pay for. His cousin refused, and suggested that he work in his firm for a year and earn the money. This refusal revived all the patient's inner conflicts with his cousin and was clearly projected as an example of injustice. A somatic breakdown followed (previously the patient had always been in excellent health). That year he had an emergency appendectomy, a hernia operation, a minor complication of the testicles, and following this his first hay fever attack. It was only then, under such extreme conditions, that his mother stepped in to help, sending him to a nursing home. Jonathan had evidently felt so deprived of his mother's love that this interest in him was experienced as great kindness. (He did not relate to the obvious rejection in her sending him away rather than caring for him herself.)

After this year of illness and his mother's "kindness," he was able to move away from home. He made his first real male friend and they shared an apartment. He painted with ease and enjoyment. There was peace and happiness in this friendship that he had never found elsewhere. However, because of constant urging by his fiancee, the patient gave in, married, and moved out. Shortly after that his friend left for Paris and was never heard from again, but according to rumors became a drug addict and gradually deteriorated. Jonathan was grief-stricken. He blamed himself for having succumbed to his wife's aggressiveness. His feelings again were those of betrayal and injustice. But the situation also precipitated a new level of guilt; conviction that he had deserted his father. He was a coward for not having sided with his father in resisting humiliation by his mother, for identifying himself with his mother as a strong and domineering character. His hostility was equally great toward both parents; toward his mother for not giving him an identity, toward the father for not giving him a masculine identity.

In his daily quarrels with his wife, Jonathan re-enacted the relationship with his parents. Transference displacement was fluid. He was both mother and father; his wife too was alternately either parent. In rejecting his wife's "total demands" for "total love" he was reliving a revenge on his mother. However, these quarrels decreased as the painter began to see in them his need for attention from his mother and his deep dependency needs.

For several years the artist was in daily close contact with a younger painter whom he first met through the unusual similarity of their styles of painting.. Independently they chose similar subject matter, and their works were enough alike to have been done by the same artist. (Cousin transference figure.) A rift developed when his friend seemed to outdistance him through "unscrupulous methods." Jonathan believed the friend was stealing his ideas and was inviting gallery representatives to see only his paintings. Soon Jonathan began to feel like an outsider in his own studio, as he had always felt his father was an outsider in his own home. He spent many weeks in treatment preoccupied with this "betrayal." The feud persists to date; the other painter is now recognized as a major American artist. Jonathan believed that other artists either stole from him or in other ways deprived him of recognition due. (Acting out of his stealing act from his cousin and his cousin's robbing him of mother's affection.)

In contrast, Jonathan had areas of healthy functioning and maintaining self-esteem. He was an excellent art teacher. His schedule of teaching was heavy, with large classes. He also taught prominent professional people who saw him not only as an outstanding teacher but as a charming and witty person as well. No family quarrels interfered with this aspect of his life. However there was never any desire to remain content with this acceptance. He became more and more resentful of teaching and regarded it as another injustice that robbed him of his time and right to paint.

The patient also used his warm and fatherly personality as a means of retaining self-esteem. There was a genuineness about this which made for him many devoted friends—particularly motherly women. In the home it became complicated by a confusion of parental roles; was he father or mother? This added another feeling of injustice, that he was not looked up to as "the father" in his own home. He did not realize that he negated his own position by a teasing, sadistic humor that disrupted his warmth, particularly to his daughter.

One of the first concrete activities in treatment was completion of a successful business venture, purchase of a multiple dwelling in a small town near the city, to be used for living quarters—with a studio nearby—and as a source of income from rentals. He discovered that he could handle business matters with skill and ability. At the same time, he felt, masochistically, that his fellow artists now regarded him as a businessman rather than a painter.

Dreams were used throughout treatment. At first Jonathan confirmed, in dreams, his feelings of injustice and betrayal. Gradually he saw how he used this defense, as well as others, to guard against real feelings of fear, guilt, hostility, and envy. He then began to use dreams in two ways: to clarify his conflicts, and to withdraw from them by denying and detaching himself from his own dreams. This defense became a working tool in treatment. He recognized that this detachment occurred whenever new awareness became threatening. Periods of non-dreaming were usually periods of even greater resistance during which the therapist became a new transference figure preliminary to working through the next stage of conflict.

The artist also began to see in his dreams a parallel between conflicts and painting difficulties. Quarrels with his wife were begun anew each day, as if the previous day's quarrel had not existed. He was always "betrayed" by her warmth after she had "humiliated" him. In his paintings too there was no continuity or growth. Each day's painting was a new beginning, as if he had never painted before. He could not build on experience—he could not find a style of his own—he could bring to resolution neither a painting nor a quarrel.

There were many dreams of guilt, in which he felt his crimes were major ones yet he didn't know what they were. He felt watched, judged, and found wanting. In his painting he felt his style was awkward and ponderous; he was compelled to balance light and dark, strong values and weak, one form with another. Unless the paintings were labored and made these adjustments they were ineffectual. Objectively the patient could see these painting adjustments were arbitrary, taking away from spontaneity and creativity.

Jonathan expressed feelings of inadequacy and guilt about body image in many dreams of rituals in which focus was on their trance-like, compulsive quality. (In a dream of an initiation ritual of urination, his genital was awkward and he splattered the wall with urine. In another dream a friend criticized the small size of his genital, as he, in reality, did to his painting.) The artist could not paint nude figures without feeling uneasy; the few he completed he could not exhibit.

Every area of conflict was reflected in inhibitions of creative efforts. Jonathan did not feel he had a right to sign his name to his paintings—the signature did not seem to be his own since the family name belonged to his cousin too. He always experienced uneasiness in exhibiting and hanging his paintings; being assertive in this way was equated with aggression and hostility. In having to deny this hostility, he denied any decisive feelings about his painting from one level of denial to another, extending to the final one—that they were not his paintings.

He was so debilitated and fatigued from inner conflict that he used psychosomatic conditions as aids to strength. Diabetes was the chief illness. His doctor was puzzled by this and regarded it as atypical. The patient could literally see each morning his equilibrium resetablished with the daily insulin injections. He reassured himself by daily doses of energy proportionate to his debilitation.

There were many dreams with anal content directly expressing hostility and confusion about passivity and feminine identification. (In dreams things were backward, in reverse, upside down. Things weren't what they should be, so that judgment was confused.) The patient could see how all this was reflected in his lack of judgment, his inability to be decisive. He was never sure whether his work was good or bad. Sometimes a painting would seem very good, the next day it would look terrible and he would destroy it. Bound within, as he was, the painting could not be free of guilt and awkwardness. It had no decisiveness or identity as he had felt no identity as a child.

As the situation with his mother became clarified, and as primitive oral dependency needs and anal hostility were worked through in treatment, Jonathan became ready to focus on the phallic period of establishing his masculinity. As he shifted dependency feelings to his father and identified with him, Jonathan developed asthma. He expressed this as he phoned his mother and told her triumphantly he had his father's asthma. But the identification made him fearful, because his father had been weak and ineffectual.

Somatically the diabetes had been normal for weeks without injections, as he worked through dependency needs for his mother. Now, as the father with asthma, the patient felt in danger of becoming an invalid who mustn't exert or excite himself. His identification with his father was a passive, feminine one. Homosexual fears developed. There were numerous dreams of men, both homosexual passive men, and strong aggressive men (men to give him injections of strength.)

The artist began at that time to shift from painting to drawing. The drawings were completed rapidly and decisively; there was much productivity. He was awed by this flow and didn't know where the content derived from. They were highly intellectualized, symbolic renditions of man's emotional struggle to survive and achieve freedom. It was as if the patient were re-enacting his own and his father's emotional history with all the yearning inherent in the love from the father. He held his first one-man exhibition in many years, and it was warmly received in the art world. Drawing, however, was experienced as an inferior art. Drawing was to painting as his passive father was to his dominating mother. Painting was still symbolically the creative expression of the powerful female.

The patient gradually regained his health. Asthma waned. Diabetes, for the first time in years, was normal. He went off insulin, went on a strict diet and lost thirty pounds. (A healthy ego control instead of injections.)

He felt equal to his cousin, who began to relate to him as a peer and discussed his own complaints about his aunt. He said he felt as if at last he had attained his manhood.

The hostile, oral dependency on the "devouring mother" (so seen in terms of patient's primitive needs for her and hostility to her) had decreased, and freed of much need for and guilt about her, Jonathan formed a strong attachment to a young woman. He related his sexual affair in a detached way—the more involving fantasy lay within his deep longing for this youthful counterpart of his newly found youthful self. He acted out being adolescent, made close friends in a group of adolescents, had parties for them. He lived out in his relationship with his young girl friend his daughter's first sexual affair. He preferred to be among the young.

Creatively the artist was able to make new beginnings, with new forms, new styles. Emphasis had shifted from the compulsion to always begin again, with no feeling of continuity, to the joy and hope of new beginnings and their continuity.

The patient repudiated all feelings of depression, repetition and dullness. The obsessional quality of the helpless, trapped feelings, and the masochistic complaints had lost their roots. He repudiated his own mourning of old age. He brought in a caricature of himself done by his cousin at the funeral of Jonathan's father. He commented that he (the patient) looked like an old beggar, coming to dance at the funeral. He was no longer the father who needed the mother—he was the adolescent boy beginning his adolescent independence. He was quite manic in his new-felt youthfulness. He went to a Picasso exhibit with his girl friend and felt there was no question but that he, too, had qualities of flexibility and fluidity. He might even become as great a painter as Picasso.

In dreams Jonathan fluctuated between masculine and feminine identification. He dreamt he was pregnant, and then was actually giving birth. In the acting-out relationship with his girl friend, he felt he was all things, as strong as a man, as tender as a woman. So too, in his painting, there was no longer the fear of no resolution, or of not having a particular style (previous obsessional complaints) but the manic feeling that he could be, and paint, anything. His paintings belonged to him as did his name, his particular style of painting, etc. He began painting elongated figures instead of the previous squat ones. He also freely exhibited his new paintings. Again there was very close correlation between healthy ego functioning and painting.

The patient experienced the cumulative effect of release of crippling defenses in a manic quality of health. But the early deprivation of love in childhood had built a personality foundation of inadequacy feelings and weakness. He leaned heavily on the therapist throughout treatment for acceptance, which he experienced as love. He was still fearful of finding his own strength in his own growth. He was used to a dependency orientation and once more sought this in trying to see his father as a strong figure.

The patient's affair of adolescence waned. When his wife threatened to leave, he acted out the mistress-lover, bought her expensive gifts, etc. There was a new level of identification with his father as an attractive lover. He recalled that his father had been married previously. He also vividly recalled his deep attachment for an uncle, his father's brother, who always treated him with great warmth and love. He had gone as far as he could in masculine identification.

With this feeling of strength the patient's asthma completely disappeared. But the attempt to make his father into a strong character gave way to reality, and he became fearful, and began to regress. His father had died when he was 22. Would he too die when his daughter was 22? He began again to see wife and mother as the strong woman figures. His father died, his mother survived and was still energetic. Diabetes recurred at the highest point it had ever been. He dreamt of himself as an Amazon woman with breastplates. This period of regression was a brief one, lasting several weeks.

He could clearly see this attempt to gain strength from identification with a strong father figure. This need subsided, as relieved of inner conflict, Jonathan began to feel healthy and energetic. Fatigue and all other somatic complaints were infrequent. He found new strength in the reality of gratifying, positive situations that now seemed to be everywhere. There was peace at home with his wife, and excellent relations with daughter, mother and cousin.

There was a new acceptance by fellow artists. He was recognized by them as a fellow painter on their serious professional level, seeking, as they were, new forms of self expression. There has been a steady flow of productivity. Jonathan has now had several annual shows. He has sold paintings consistently and has gained from the art world acceptance and good predictions for his future.

Predictions

Prediction #1

The patient projects tendencies to exploit, to be unfair, to steal ideas, upon his colleagues. This deprives him of their emotional support and friendship. Over and above this, he is so immersed in his projections that he does not have sufficient energy for work. He puts all family matters ahead of work. *When his unconscious projections and the parallel hostilities have been worked through, this man will have considerably more energy available for work. It is questionable, however, how far this energy will carry him.*

Results: *The patient did considerably better than the prediction suggests. He became an extremely productive artist, with a notable verve and joyousness in his approach to his work and its execution.*

Prediction #2

Sado-masochistic trends permeate the personality, leading to constant strife, quarrels and longing for warmth from the very person (especially his wife) against whom the patient protests and complains. Again this drains his energy and leaves too little for creative work. *The sado-masochistic tendencies are so com-*

plex, so intense, and so long-standing that it is questionable whether we can wholly free the patient's energy for work.

Results: *The patient went far beyond the prediction. Already in the second year of treatment—when he turned temporarily from painting to drawing—his creative work proceeded with an enthusiasm and rapidity that were unprecedented.*

Prediction #3

The patient suffers from intense feelings of guilt, prompted in large measure by the damned-up hostility, mainly toward his cousin. Specifically he cannot forgive himself—and here we deal with conscious feelings—for the theft of a painting done by his cousin, which he presented as his own and for which he received acclaim. As a result, he feels his own paintings are not his, and should not bear his signature. 1) *When this incident is specifically worked through and placed in the past, the patient will look on his work with respect and a true sense of ownership.* 2) *Other progress will depend on the degree to which all-pervasive hostility can be made conscious and consequently be reduced. We expect good results.*

Results: *The patient exceeded the "good" results envisaged.*

Prediction #4

The patient has great hostility towards the female and the female genital specifically. He transfers this to his paintings, which he regards as Indians regard the scalps they hang on the walls. By transferring hostility in this manner to his paintings, the patient devalues them. *It is expected that this specific stream of hostility can be worked through and that the patient will cease to equate paintings with female organs, hung like trophies on walls.*

Results: *This prediction came true entirely.*

Prediction #5

Out of hostility, the patient covers over completed canvases, destroying them in the careful manner that is in keeping with his obsessive-compulsive defenses. *If we can reduce hostility sufficiently, this preservative form of destruction will cease.*

Results: *Total success; the patient ceased to "hide" his paintings behind new coats of paint.*

Prediction #6

The patient's body image is to him an unattractive one and he injects this feeling into the nude figures he draws. The patient experiences his genitals as too small and ineffectual. He feels similarly disappointed and uneasy about his human figures. *When his body image changes, his feelings for the figures he draws will change.* Results: *Completely successful. The patient developed a zest for drawing nude figures.*

Directions of Development and Ratings

Dynamics

1. Passive-hostile, especially towards mother and wife — attachment with other female figures—assertive (8)
2. Sado-masochistic — emergence of manic feelings — self-esteem and self-affirmation (8)
3. Unconscious competitiveness — projection of competitiveness on others — gradual insight — co-operative (9)
4. Guilt feelings — manic feelings of non-guilt — truly free of guilt (9)
5. Feminine identification — homosexual fears — pregnancy fantasies — masculine identification (8)
6. Intellectualization —affective relationships (7.5)
7. Obsessiveness — inner freedom (7.5)
8. Asthma, hay fever — free from asthma (9)
9. Atypical diabetes — diabetes disappeared (9)
10. New quarrels each day with central figures — experience of continuity of good feelings (8.5)

Work Patterns

I. Unable to concentrate on work—concentration (9)
II. Feeling estranged from work (reluctant to sign it) — at one with work (signs it) (9)
III. Oppressed by criticism of others — relying on self evaluation (9)
IV. No sense of identity — sense of identity (8.5)
V. Covering over finished canvasses — finishing many works (9)
VI. Inability to work through whole canvas—working through whole canvas (9)
VII. Compelled to ponderous approach to work — paints lightly and fluidly (9)
VIII. New start each day — continuity (9)
IX. Rigidity in balance and form — freedom (9)
X. Not exhibiting — exhibiting freely (9)

Discussion of Size and Distribution of Ratings

The ratings given to the Directions of Development both in the area of dynamics and of work patterns reflect conspicuous improvement in this patient. Along all directions the development goes well beyond the mid-point (five). This is not just a "good" improvement, indicating that someone has been helped through treatment to function adequately. Rather, looking at the picture the ratings present, we note that this individual has achieved the utmost recovery along four out of nine areas in the dynamics field, and that in nine out of ten areas in the work pattern field he has gone to the optimal point of nine. Those directions to which lesser than optimal ratings are assigned also reflect very good development, for these ratings too are uniformly high. It is interesting to note that the lowest ratings, as in the case of Matthew Taylor (the first case presented), are assigned to movement along the direction of intellectualization and obsessiveness.

Both in the area of dynamics and the area of work patterns the spread of improvement is not segmental but total, for not just a few of the Directions of Development reflect progress, but each and every one shows a conspicuous gain. By definition this means that nowhere was there any arrestation or backward movement. Here, then, is the second case in which we note that in the field in which we are specifically interested, that of the patient's work patterns, psychoanalytic psychotherapy did not have any adverse effect. It most certainly did not drain the patient with regard to the energy and the modes with which he approached his work. On the contrary, the improvement appears remarkably deep and far-reaching.

This patient, so the Directions of Development show, is a man who produces much more work than before (see work pattern direction VI). He can now concentrate fully, whereas previously he could not (see work pattern direction I), and despite some remnants of obsessiveness in the personal dynamics (see dynamics direction 7) the rigidity in balance and form, previously quite considerable, has given way to full freedom (see work pattern direction IX). In sum, then, we can say that creativity as measured by work patterns, the only aspect with which we are concerned in this study, far from being adversely affected, flourished.

When we compare the changes in dynamics with the changes in work patterns we are able to make a number of connections. The guilt feelings which dynamics direction 4 connotes as having been worked out completely correspond to the painter's cessation of feeling estranged from his work, which he felt he did not deserve and did not feel free to sign, and to his new experience of being one with his work and signing it readily. Too, the considerable, though not total, lessening of intellectualization and obsessiveness is undoubtedly connected with the development towards a light and fluid manner of painting (see work pattern direction VII), and the new freedom that has replaced the previous need for a rigid approach to balance and form (see work pattern direction IX). The cessation of daily quarrels which, according to the patient's own words "chopped up" his life (see dynamics direction 10) appears directly connected with the emerging continuity in work, as reflected in work pattern direction VIII. This continuity in work consisted of a reinstatement day by day of similar or identical feelings toward the canvases worked on, so that the patient completed canvases which he previously would have painted over many times.

Changes of Work Patterns

Jonathan Norton, more than any of the other creative subjects in our project, sought treatment because of the multiple work blocks from which he suffered and which had virtually choked off all ability to start and complete paintings. In his other areas of activity, teaching and administering the daily life of his family and himself, this man functioned well, even when he entered treatment. In appearance, manner, social relating, and self-image, the patient regarded himself as the "father type" to whom people bring *their* problems. He had been an excellent art teacher for years. His classes were well attended; it was his major source of income.

During the first period of treatment, the patient sustained this self-image of independence by his purchase of a multiple dwelling, handling complex financial matters astutely and maturely.

He had daily quarrels with his wife, and had woven his intensely competitive and hostile feelings into a somewhat paranoid system which he projected upon colleagues to the point where they cut him off. However, unlike the other individuals under study here, his primary purpose in coming to treatment was not to improve his life situation. He functioned quite planfully in this area. What he felt as gravely threatened—and indeed it was—was his life as a creative artist.

At the beginning of treatment Jonathan was unable totally to concentrate on his creative work. Any family matter that distracted his attention was only too welcome and received priority. He spent his time marketing, setting up his studio in different ways, and attending to all needs of wife and daughter. Underlying this "pull away from work" were enormous slumbering hostilities interlocked with sado-masochistic patterns. The patient was totally unaware of these trends, which were deeply repressed, the energy necessary to maintain the repressions making a free and serious absorption in work impossible.

Dream interpretations were extremely helpful in making the patient aware of the extent to which his passivity and masochism were a cover-up for aggression. Almost as soon as there resulted a more openly hostile approach to the central figures—mother and wife—a freeing of energy for work was observed. The patient began to work intensively, although interestingly enough on drawings rather than paintings, thus steeping himself in work that was less emotionally toned. He was later able to transfer these new bursts of activity and energy to his paintings. The patient was awed and amazed at this burst of activity. He did not know where it came from as he himself did not as yet make the connection between the "unfreezing" and the change in passive, sado-masochistic patterns. The drawings produced were beautifully executed, technical pieces, symbolic renditions of man's fight to survive poverty, suppression, confusion. Gradually these drawings became larger and more powerful as the hostility became increasingly more open.

In his second year of treatment, he looked forward to an exhibition of his work, because he was convinced—periods of pessimism granted—that the flow of energy would last. When periodically his productivity would lessen, the old tendency to do all kinds of other things was less in evidence. Rather, he studied his finished works and those of other painters, his mind preoccupied with painting and not taking flight into other areas.

At times now the patient complains to his therapist and to friends that he does not produce during periods which are actually very productive and during which many works are sold. In the third year of treatment a new style emerged, characterized by a new strength previously not present.

The continually growing concentration on work is illustrated by an incident towards the end of treatment. The patient contemplated taking time away from his work to attend the funeral of a friend, entailing travel to another part of the country. He decided that this would represent a return to his previous tendency to give priority to matters other than his creative activities. He did not go, but instead did a painting in memory of his friend which he entitled "Conclusion." The rating of nine in work pattern direction I reflects the enormous progress made in this work habit.

This painter's life at the beginning of therapy was literally haunted by the shadow of his cousin, gifted and favored. In his first struggling years as an artist the patient took one of his cousin's paintings, showed it at an exhibition, and won a prize. Today, looking at that painting, he realizes that it is not really a fine piece of work. However, the incident had lingered in his memory as representative of the murderous rivalry felt towards the cousin, and his attempt to be successful. The effect of it could not be wiped out except through psychoanalytic therapy, where the roots of the theft were analyzed and removed.

The hostility towards the cousin, until it was brought out into the open, lead to an interesting defense. All kinds of destruction and "breaking" had to be avoided. The patient felt intellectually that he must break accepted forms, but rigid defenses kept him from doing so in imagery. He said, "I can't go so far as to destroy the concept of the human image. I fear doing it. Yet to move on I must destroy the structure I have created. I shall feel estranged from my work as long as this barrier keeps me from going ahead with a blast where a blast should be."

After some tentative breaking of form, the patient went back once more to a gentleness he knew did not coincide with his inner feelings. Finally the strength broke through. The rivalry with the cousin was settled, the two had become good friends. Jonathan felt a close personal identification with his paintings. Work pattern direction II, with the rating of nine, reflects this total reversal from estrangement from his work to a sense of union with it.

The patient, at first totally unaware of his intense hostilities, had no idea of the causes behind his compulsion to paint over finished canvases, even those he liked. In the second year of treatment he had a fierce quarrel with his wife. He went to the studio and took out two canvases. One represented two men, one locked in a cave, the other embracing a basket of fruit. The second painting showed a woman bathing. The patient recognized that the two men were himself, and that the woman represented his wife. He painted over both canvases, although they were paintings he admired. In discussing this incident in treatment, he was able to see that it was rage that made him paint over finished works many times, thus depriving him of results. The habit totally disappeared, as the rating of nine on work pattern direction V shows.

At first Jonathan acted as an outcast among his peers, which indeed his conduct had considerably justified. Repeated expressions of suspicion had alienated people from him. Moreover, his sharply reduced output had drawn comments of a negative nature. The patient felt he was derided, unwanted. He invited criticisms from some people, such as the painter B.C., a prominent and paternalistic man. Eventually the patient ceased to invite constructive criticism, and if it came nevertheless, he made it clear that it was unwanted. He came to rely much more on his own evaluations, which he compared with those of others, without permitting the comments of his colleagues to prevail on him with resultant pessimism and inactivity.

The patient experienced, in the beginning of treatment, little identity in his work. He felt he had no style. Whatever was characteristic of him was caught in obsesssional details but not in any major form of painting. He was ashamed of the fluctuations of sexual identity which his dreams began to reflect, some representing him as male, some as female. He knew that what he was, and what he painted, was neither fish nor fowl. Gradually this changed. The patient moved towards a state where he felt he was as strong as a man and as tender as a woman. This he accepted within himself and carried into his paintings. Now he felt he could paint everything. Indeed he did paint everything. This was not evidence of having no identity but of possessing a truly wide range of feelings. A manic period followed where the patient painted in new styles, and took to new subject matter. This was followed by a more quiet experience of having a rich style all his own, changing yet with cores of identity. The direction of development IV shows that the judges considered the progress toward a personal identity nearly complete, giving this dimension a rating of 8.5.

The obsessional personal dynamics did much to interfere with work. The patient complained constantly that he could not work through a whole canvas, that he was obsessed with part aspects but not able to evolve an overall structure. Connected with this was a lack of fluidity. He described an awkwardness of hand and style which he took pains to conceal. The act of concealing the awkwardness consumed more energy than the act of making new forms. He remarked that the preoccupation with detail and the awkward heaviness stemmed from the smallness of his nature, which he felt to be hemmed in. As hostility broke forth, the changes became notable. There was greater fluidity and a movement into all directions, away from "sitting in the corners of details."

The patient said that his paintings took on the character of free associations; ideas, forms, colors streamed out of him, sometimes almost against his will. For instance, he painted in one canvas a male figure and then there came out of him a female one alongside the male. He said: "The female figure is as though from another era. This makes me angry because it is different from what I want. But I must admit the painting is very good."

Formerly squat and tight forms now became elongated. The artist developed a new pallette of brighter colors.

As the preoccupation with detail and the heaviness disappeared high moods developed. The figures looked to the artist like "spring." We see that both the movement away from detail towards the whole canvas and the path from awkwardness to light and fluid handling of work is reflected by two top ratings. Work pattern directions VI and VII are rated with nine. Furthermore, direction IX shows a movement from rigidity to freedom which is connected with the above developments and is also optimal.

When Jonathan was first seen, he felt that both his time and his life were chopped up. As his days were fragmented by quarrels with his wife that never settled anything, so too he worked in bits and pieces. Each day brought different and often conflicting ideas so that daily he started out to work anew. He completed almost nothing. Each painting, he reported, was a new beginning, but not in a good sense. He started each day and each painting with the feeling that he had never painted before. Then, in the second year of treatment, there was a new feeling of joy. He developed a sense of continuity. Moreover, with one painting finished, he could now use the knowledge acquired, the perfection found, the visual images, for variations in other paintings. He could connect his paintings.

The artist had sold very few paintings when he started therapy. He was ashamed to sell them on a social basis, and the galleries were less and less eager to represent him because his work had shown no development. Moreover, his suspicious attitude had estranged many gallery owners. The patient stated that he sold himself whenever he sold a painting, and he did not think he was worth selling.

Subsequently, he held two one-man shows, and though he told everyone he was doing badly, the facts indicated quite the opposite. At the end of treatment the artist was looking forward to his third one-man show, predicting that it would be a great success (which it was). Again, compare these statements with work pattern direction X having a rating of nine, which reflects the great extent to which the patient was helped in emerging from what was tantamount to a creative standstill.

CHAPTER 5

The Case of Tina Mandell, a Painter

Case Report

TINA MANDELL entered treatment at the age of twenty-five. She had exhibited two oil paintings, several collages and some ink drawings in three group shows. Her ink drawings and collages were acclaimed as fine pieces of art with a primitive Etruscan feeling to them. The artist taught at two Art Centers and devoted her spare time to her own work. She was deeply resentful over the necessity to teach, caused by meagre finances. Tina would have preferred to spend all free time in her studio on her own work.

Tina had married four months before she came to treatment and was under the impression that she cared deeply for her husband, a weak and ineffectual man who had difficulty holding on to jobs. He was a writer and worked intermittently in various publishing houses as an editor. His small salary was whittled away before he brought it home, because as soon as he was paid he would go on buying sprees and purchase fine tobacco, prints and old books. It turned out relatively soon that Tina harbored many repressed resentments over the poorly-managed budget situation, and over the unreliability of her husband, who did not keep his promises, misplaced his belongings and had no direction in his professional life. Severe anxiety attacks which were the presenting symptom that prompted the patient to seek treatment were in considerable measure due to the impact upon the patient's weak defenses and poorly-established ego functions of the extremely bad marital situation. Specifically there was the patient's unconscious fear that she might abandon her husband or that her rage against him might lead her to act against

[76]

him and injure him. The picture was that of a schizophrenic person with inadequate defenses, regressed in many areas of functioning and given to many primitive mechanisms such as excessive identifications and incorporation tendencies.

Tina was graceful and lovely. Although she was told by her parents, by girl friends and by many men that she was extremely attractive, her image of herself was rather confused. She was able at times to acknowledge her beauty, yet soon after would experience herself as unattractive. When people looked at her, which was often the case on account of her lovely features and lovely facial expression she often mistook such glances as expressions of contempt and derision. This tied up with other paranoid tendencies which were clearly demonstrated. Tina believed that critics were unfair to her, that gallery owners wished to take advantage, and that older painters ridiculed her, although in actuality she was given an unusually positive reception for an artist who was just establishing herself.

The chief symptom, as mentioned, was acute and prolonged anxiety. During the first five months of treatment the patient was more often anxiety ridden than not. The anxiety was expressed in part in a variety of physical symptoms, such as fast breathing, perspiration, and motoric restlessness which drove her to walk fast through the streets and made it impossible for her to paint since work demanded a higher degree of motoric coordination and calm than Tina was able to muster. The restless state of the body was accompanied by a somewhat manic mental condition. Thoughts of subjectively bewildering variety raced through her head, and she had difficulty articulating them clearly. The patient, as we see, was holding on to her defenses by a slim margin and was close to a breakdown, although she managed to function fairly well in her teaching, less well yet still acceptably as a homemaker, and pretty well in social situations.

Tina was fairly well aware of several other emotional constellations that indicated malfunctioning and which she wished sincerely to change and improve. She was given to a degree of identification which was pathological and conspicuous. She "became" the person she was with, assuming the other person's gestures and the other's mood. This was true especially when she was with a person who suffered or towards whom Tina felt hostile or even mildly antipathetic. This artist bore out a condition described by Bychowski (2). Bychowski raises the point that artists tend to "have especially mobile cathexes and counter-cathexes and that these extend to the ego boundaries as well, leading to an extraordinary faculty of the creative ego for multiple identifications." Bychowski's point that "this extends beyond human beings so that the artist seems to penetrate (through his identifications) into the mysteries and essence of things" was applicable to this young painter. She was able, upon reading about a period of history and looking at some art works of the period, to reach into the spirit of that time with great exactness and intensity.

Tina was also concerned about her tendency to withdraw her affect and attention from others as soon as they brought some unwelcome pressure to bear on her. While she often felt strong love for her husband and her younger sister who, as we shall see played a special role in Tina's life, she withdrew from either for long periods of time, seemingly in automatic fashion without intervention of conscious will on her part. The patient, whose conscience was very severe, especially where any breach of love was concerned, felt guilt-stricken when she was overcome, as it were, by the withdrawal mechanism. She suffered for the person whom she had abandoned through her withdrawal. She experienced her withdrawal as a sense of darkness descending upon the person whom she withdrew from and on herself.

In the early phases of treatment the artist alternated between good relationships with other painters, gallery owners and friends and feelings of suspicion and distrust. She was suspicious of and hostile to the therapist. She was not sure she was being helped. She had dreams in which the therapist's office appeared dirty and the furniture smashed, or else the office was hidden from her. This suspicion was followed by gradually growing trust and confidence which eventually became the basis for many relationships.

When the patient entered treatment she was as involved with her parents, both of whom were relatively young and healthy, as most individuals are before adolescence. Her parents often helped her financially; they took her to the physician if she needed a check-up and she spent many vacation days with them. In fact it soon became clear that the unhappy marriage Tina had undertaken, which was one of the motivating forces of the anxiety condition, constituted an attempt on Tina's part to emancipate herself from the engulfing, unhappy, erotically-overcharged relationship with both parents. Tina was the favorite child of both mother and father. The parents had four children; Tina was third oldest. Her mother, who had many erotic leanings toward the female sex, loved Tina psysically to a degree that was very theatening to the patient. The father in turn had many pet names for her that indicated a sexually loaded relationship and he touched her and kissed her without restraint.

An outstanding problem in the relationship with both parents, as well as with the other three siblings, was the fact that thoughts and feelings between the parents themselves and between parents and children remained unarticulated, unaired and often concealed. The passionate and conflicting emotional currents were expressed when the patient was alone with one parent. Moreover, many practical details of day-to-day living remained undisclosed. The artist, for example, did not know at the time she entered treatment what sort of work her father did nor what his financial circumstances were. She had almost no memories of her childhood and adolescent years. Only in the fourth year of treatment did Tina discover to her surprise and relief that her father was substantially insured and that he had large holdings of real estate and stock. In the third year she began to recall early memories.

The lack of articulation that predominated in the parental household related to Tina's productivity and to her use of art as a means of survival. She often said that she was lacking in verbal means of communication. This was not entirely untrue, although at times her choice of words was excellent and precise. At such times the discernment for modes of verbal expression was as fine as her choice of material, color and form in painting. Yet such occasions of verbal fluency and precision were infrequent, and more often the artist experienced a subjectively frightening inability to capture and articulate her feelings in words. At such times the ability to turn to the non-verbal media of painting and drawing reinforced her sense of sanity.

Parental authority generally was wielded over Tina and her three siblings in an inarticulate, indirect way. The parents did not come out clearly with their expectations, and punishments consisted not of predictable and circumscribed measures but in the form of a silent withdrawal of love. The only area in which authority was expressed directly was in the area of cleanliness. The mother, especially, was a fiend where neatness and cleanliness were concerned. Attempts were made to toilet train Tina early and a great deal of neatness in room and clothes was expected. The patient defied her mother's arduous demands stubbornly. Early childhood games, which she only remembered vaguely, seem to have focused on expressing opposition to her mother's neatness. She played with mud, and covered the surfaces of the walls with doodles and pictures. Here was an artist whose motivation to paint stemmed clearly in part from original anal yearnings and a continuation of the child's early infatuation with the tactile quality of excrements. The fight between mother and daughter was carried into adult life. Because of partly conscious, partly unconscious defiance of her mother's standards Tina remained a conspicuously untidy person.

The patient's opposition to neatness and her fascination for the unclean were expressed in her appearance. Although she was a beautiful, slender, tall girl with fine features and a peaches and cream skin, she looked disheveled during the first and second year of treatment. Her hair was untidy, unwashed and untrimmed. Even her neck was at times unclean and her clothes, though interestingly matched as far as colors were concerned, were often stained and wrinkled. The confused self image mentioned earlier stemmed in part from Tina's feeling that she was "a dirty little girl" and as such unacceptable to anyone but herself.

A factor in the anxiety attacks from which Tina suffered when she began therapy was the nervous breakdown her youngest sibling had just three weeks before the onset of Tina's anxiety. Her sister Rachel broke down after her fiancee suddenly left her, and had to be committed to a mental hospital.

Tina was only eleven months older than her sister, who had been an unwanted child and whom the parents rejected in many ways, always comparing her unfavorably with the older, brighter, prettier and more capable Tina. From an early age Tina allowed Rachel to become her charge. She took her to school, consoled her when other children made fun because she was awkward, and directly and mostly executed Rachel's homework.

From an early age Tina directed toward Rachel a complex network of mental and emotional processes: she identified with Rachel, often feeling that the other children's sneers and teachers' criticisms were directed at her rather than at Rachel. As a result her own sense of identity was badly impaired; she was never quite sure where the provinces of her own functioning ended and where Rachel's began. Tina loved Rachel in one sense, but on the other hand she resented her and the burden the parents imposed by rejecting Rachel and leaving her upbringing and protection to Tina.

Tina tried to make up for her repressed resentments by taking Rachel's suffering upon herself. By *being* Rachel, by feeling as though she were herself the inferior younger sister, she tried to make amends to the girl she often unconsciously wished were not there.

When she entered treatment, Tina knew that her relationship with her sister was "wrong," though she was unable to clarify to herself just what were the pathological factors. She knew that she was much too involved with her sister, and that despite the involvement there was an absence of real love. She suspected that this relationship served as a pattern for all her other relationships. This was quite true, since as we have seen, she identified to an excessive and destructive degree with any person who suffered.

The patient's relationship with her husband soon turned out to be patterned in many respects along the same lines as the sister prototype. Her husband, an ineffectual, dependent, frightened man, rarely worked. The few jobs that he landed he lost very soon. He was often late for work, fought with superiors, and suffered from depressions that seriously affected his abilities. Tina suffered her husband's defeats as though they were her own. When these extraordinary identification tendencies began to be corrected in treatment, her anxiety subsided gradually until in the second year of treatment it disappeared. This was accompanied by a temporary change in personality. Instead of her usual sad, yielding behavior, Tina displayed a demanding and fierce front. This lasted about six months. She asked her husband to manage his finances better, to keep his appointments and to take a firmer and clearer stand on personal and professional issues. When he failed to come through, she began to consider divorce.

The described fierceness ended when the artist began to get in touch with her deeper feelings, especially her intense love of nature, of fruits, flowers and stone formations, all of which she studied, collected and frequently used as subject matters of her creative work. The original softness returned, but anxiety remained lessened. Toward the end of the fourth year of treatment there were only the briefest twinges of occasional anxiety.

Previously when Tina suffered from anxiety for extended periods she could not contemplate working and did not go near her studio. Since she needed movement, particularly pacing and walking, to master the anxiety, the confinement of the studio was frightening. Free from anxiety for increasingly longer periods, she resumed her work with fervor and only stayed away from the studio during spells of mild anxiety. She produced drawings and paintings of such quality as well as quantity that she had her first one-woman show.

As Tina's energy increased and her demands became firmer her husband failed even more in his work and finally had a partial breakdown. He became increasingly anxious, refused to get up during the day, and displayed dissociation and confusion of thoughts. Tina was strongly tempted to regress to earlier tendencies of identification with the sufferer. Again she felt her husband's misery as if it were her own. A struggle between therapist and husband developed, the therapist asking that the patient maintain the progress she had made, the husband drawing her back and trying to inflict his pain on her. At the end of the crisis the husband went abroad for two months. When he returned, Tina had extricated herself from this unhappy relationship and convinced him of the necessity of a divorce. It is interesting to note that the next man with whom she fell in love was a rather weak man. Their relation lasted for six months. Tina's next love was an effective, accomplished, fairly strong and independent person. The sister prototype relationship had ceased to influence her choice in this case. The man Tina now loved had no serious handicaps from which she felt compelled to rescue him. There were few identifications with him.

Although Tina's love for this man was strong and deep, she was reluctant, except for a brief period early in the relationship, to marry him and set up a home. Her sexual responsiveness had increased greatly, and there was affection, passion, and intellectual companionship in this relationship. But the artist, now much stronger and with a slowly-acquired identity of her own, wished to live by herself and was happiest when her main focus was on creative work. She believed that she might eventually bridge these two worlds, her love and her art.

Towards the end of treatment Tina's attitude towards the man she loved and towards marriage changed. She desired to get married and was perturbed when the man had difficulty obtaining a divorce from his wife, from whom he had been separated for a long time. Knowing that she could live in marriage without pathological dependency and identifications, Tina was confident that she could integrate married life and an existence as a productive artist into a well-joined experience. When she terminated treatment she was not yet married, however.

In view of the extraordinary tendency to identify with others, which was focal to her personality until corrected through therapy, it is interesting to note that this artist's work was very original. This was her own conviction and was shared by those who wrote about her work. She did not copy other artists, and felt no temptation to fall into the paths of others. Her intactness in her work seemed complete. The neurotic pattern of identification which permeated her day-to-day conduct did not intrude into the work patterns. We shall see that in other respects too, the neurotic patterns did not affect her activities. Perhaps this was why she could not bring herself for so long to span the domestic and creative areas. The therapist, while helping her to achieve deeper levels of affection and a far more passionate sexual life, felt in this period that the intuitive preference for a single life should not be questioned. For it appeared virtually impossible for Tina to sustain the serenity and isolation in which creativity flourished if there were any intrusions from the world of everyday life.

With regard to the withdrawal tendencies, soon after treatment began the withdrawal—consisting of silence and a shutting off of any affect towards the external world—took an artistically productive turn. Tina had a studio roughly twenty minutes from home. When her husband disappointed her by not showing up at home at a time agreed upon, when he failed to keep other commitments and promises or squandered the little money they had, Tina at first had merely a sense of darkness descending upon her and a wish to be alone. She would then go to her studio and sit there, removed from the world. But soon the picture changed. When Tina entered the studio she became highly active. Ideas, forms, shapes, color combinations, a complex network of inspirations descended on her, and she set to work. Often she worked into the early morning hours. She felt enjoyment on the one hand and on the other, guilt for having deserted her husband or others close to her geographically and emotionally. This sense of guilt was deep, and even reporting it to the therapist caused Tina sadness. Her eyes, when she spoke of her periods of refuge in the studio, saddened, she averted her glance, lowered her lids, and her voice trailed off until it was barely audible. Throughout the first two years of psychotherapy the creation of artistic work was accompanied by guilt, and viewing her work the artist also felt guilty because it had been produced in secrecy and in a mood that expressed hostility towards and withdrawal from the central persons in her life.

In examining the circumstances of withdrawal and the intense accompanying guilt feelings, a number of factors seemed to play a role. For one, the patient had a primitive concept of time, much like that of a child. When she withdrew, she felt that the condition of isolation was total and everlasting. No change was perceived as impending, since Tina felt and foresaw no future. In her inner experience the person who had caused her to withdraw was eliminated completely. Remembering in therapy that she actually had returned to parents, sister, and husband over and over in the past, helped Tina to ameliorate her guilt, because she was able to obtain some expectation of resumption of contact with the person from whom she had withdrawn.

Also, since Tina always identified with the sufferer, she experienced the pain felt by the person from whom she had withdrawn, as she though, for good. Parents, sister and husband depended on her. She felt the consternation that they were bound to feel when she withdrew in order to punish them. She felt her act of withdrawal to be cruel and wrong. The increasing, healthy sense of separation between herself and others which she learned to establish through therapy helped reduce this cause of guilt. Thus, withdrawal was modified and was not accompanied by the previously-intense sense of guilt.

During treatment Tina became considerably more articulate, though it appeared, both to her and to the therapist, that words would probably never be her primary means of conveying experience. Nor did the therapist feel that being better able to verbalize would make her notably happier. She was rooted for so long and so overwhelmingly in the visual media of expression, that it seemed advisable not to steer her away drastically from this accustomed form of communication. It seemed unlikely that words would ever provide the exhilaration she experienced through visual and tactile channels of communications.

Tina became gradually aware of the reasons why lack of cleanliness held such a fascination. Yet she stubbornly continued to maintain that she was a "dirty urchin" and insisted on keeping up the neglected appearance. A change in direction of better grooming occurred briefly at the end of the third year of treatment, apparently precipitated by two jeering remarks made at an opening of a show of her work. Within a week she turned into a well groomed young woman, but this superficial change soon disappeared.

Tina's fascination with dirt, though expressed in her appearance and visible to the observer, was in her experience something secret and underground. Playing with mud as a child and with thick paint in her work was highly pleasurable, and the pleasure had to be concealed from the outside world. The pleasure derived from what appeared to Tina to be dirty substances was regarded by her as childish and condemnable. The fact that it had to be concealed greatly heightened an ever-present sense of guilt. As the artist freed herself from the infantile connections with her mother, the touch of the materials with which she worked and their consistency became increasingly separated from "feces," dirt, and unkemptness. Concomittantly the tactile sensuous experiences became even more pleasurable because the sense of guilt had disappeared.

Tina enjoyed her studio throughout therapy but she was at times terrified by the shapes she created. Capable of instigating regressive processes almost at any moment, the artist's ability to envisage new forms and then in a new ego synthesis to reach in a disciplined way for pencil and paper to sketch them was great. In Leo Bellak's most opportunely chosen words (1) Tina was a master in undertaking on the one hand a reordering "into new configurations with new boundaries" and then oscillating to the "scrutiny of the again sharply functioning adaptive forces." However once the ego was firmly reconstituted, Tina looked with fear at that which had emerged when her whole self had undergone the loosening which fertilized the imaginative sketches she created. She disclosed to the therapist with great trepidation that she considered them insane. Several discussions about the universal nature of the processes she experienced proved very helpful. She slowly began to regard her creations as exciting, and beautiful rather than "crazy."

Tina was very impractical when she entered treatment and her sense of well being, her success and her work suffered from her inability to organize her life effectively. She was often cheated out of money by employers for whom she did menial services on a part-time basis, and she and her husband had barely enough to eat. She was paid inadequately for the teaching she did. Her studio was broken into and her work and phonograph records were stolen. As such matters came up for discussion in therapy and the connections with the past understood, she became more careful in conducting her affairs. Her teaching, the sales of her work, the setting up of a studio, planning for exhibitions—all these affairs were conducted more efficiently Tina concomittantly became more optimistic and held herself in higher esteem.

Predictions

Prediction #1

The intense and, to the patient, frightening anxiety states, the primary symptom that drove her into treatment, will lessen. Specifically it has already become evident that anxiety spells will occur at less frequent intervals, that they will be of shorter duration and less intense. Concomittantly the patient's primary defense, a somewhat hectic motoric activation that drives her away from her place of work and from concentration on work will become dispensable. Probably anxiety will disappear totally. The result will be the ability to work more continuously and to produce much more.

Results:*The prediction came true. The patient still becomes depressed frequently but is not anxious. At the present time the depressions are caused primarily by the still all too swift repression of anger and subsequent turning of the anger against the self. But the anxiety, which appeared so inexplicable to the patient and thus so frightening, has disappeared. Tina works much more continuously, as a teacher but primarily as a creative artist. When she is depressed she works unusually well, since created objects are beloved substitutions for the world she gives up when she becomes depressed.*

Prediction #2

This productive and original artist who is capable of high-level creative absorption and productivity under varied conditions, except when she is in the grips of frequent anxiety spells, might cease to be so productive were she to achieve a liaison with a man her equal whom she loved. At the present time she is married to a man who drains, bores, and irritates her. He drains her by his extreme dependency and bores her because he is her inferior, both intellectually and in terms of adaptive functioning. *It is difficult to envisage a continuation of this re-*

lationship provided the patient becomes healthier. If this woman, however, should meet and team up with a man more on a par with her, her dedication to work may change. It is possible that she will put her work second and steep herself in being a companion and a mother. Her longings both for more adult emotional and sexual love and for a child are deep and strong.

Results: *This prediction came partially true. The patient divorced her husband and fell in love with a steadier, more productive and stronger man. At the end of treatment she declared herself ready to subordinate her work in some measure to her love. The man she loved was not then free to marry her and she felt occasionally that she was rejected. She submerged herself alternately in her work, looking on her love life as a secondary domain, and alternately rejected her work in a moderate though never total manner.*

Prediction #3

One of the primary causes of the artist's intense and prolonged anxiety attacks seems to be connected with her tendency to identify herself with individuals close to her, particularly after they have offended her and given her cause to resent them. The ensuing confusion of identity and confusion about the direction of aggression promotes anxiety. *It will be possible to free the patient from the propensity towards identification.*

The artist's penchant for identifications is definitely a factor that strengthens the creative drive. It makes for a kind of pantheism directed at the objects of nature, trees, seeds, blossoms, fruit and many less specific forms that the artist perceives in the natural surroundings and which inspire her work. She "makes" works of art in large measure because she wants to possess them, and thus to possess the natural forms which she loves as though they were part of herself, since she has identified with them.

Undoubtedly with the loss of the proclivities for identification, some changes are bound to appear in the creative process. The wish to possess sculptured objects as part of the desired world around the artist will cease to remain as powerful a motivating force as it is now. However, there are so many other motivating factors that the artist will undoubtedly remain highly productive. Results: This prediction appears to have come true. Together with the propensity towards identification the artist has lost her anxiety and therefore is more free to work. There is no lack of inspiration, imagination or ideas propelling her to work, even though her intense love affair often exhausts her psychic economy, as it were, for the division between love and work is not easy and she at times makes the decision to sacrifice the work. However, her productive capacity seems bottomless.

An interesting by-product of the drop in the level of identification is the patient's increased willingness to part with her work, to have it exhibited, sold or at times given away.

Prediction #4

The patient's defenses against the parents' libidinal demands on her are at present strong, but will lessen to some degree as she will be enabled to separate herself from her parents both through a firmer delineation of ego boundaries and through a more mature heterosexual love relation of her own. At present her defenses often prompt her to withdraw psysically from parents and husband (who is partially identified with them) and to go to the studio and work. Thus present defenses against oedipal involvement serve as a motivation for the creative process. The patient seeks out the "mental set" that prompts her to create. As Bellak has put it (ibid.) the mental set is often bound to the specific stimuli which a specific external setting, such as the studio, provides. Tina's defenses, then, drive her at present towards the mental set that fertilizes the creative process. It is unlikely that they will be abandoned in large measure. *It is predicted that other motivations, equally strong, will be added once the defense of withdrawal to the studio no longer is necessary.*

Results: *This prediction came largely true. The artist usually goes to her studio freely, rather than retiring to it defensively because anxiety compelled her to move into her own realm. Her studio continues to be a place that provides the mental set that starts all the dormant artistic processes. She has rearranged her studio and made it more usable and attractive, with new shelves and a few new objects of art and of nature that excite her. Instances where she is compelled to seek out isolation, especially in the studio, do still occur, however.*

Directions of Development and Ratings

Dynamics

1. Acute anxiety — intermittent anxiety — periodic rigid control and harshness — mostly anxiety-free — supple and uncontrolling (9)

2. Excessive identifications (especially with sufferer) — normal degree of identification (6.5)

3. Withdrawal from primary figures to isolation — need not withdraw (5.5)

4. Guilt accompanies withdrawal — no guilt (6.5)

5. Unconscious resentment turned against self — insight into this — resentments less frequent, overt (7)

6. Dirt and self neglect libidinized — lowering of this cathexis (6.5)

7. Self image of an unattractive person — new self image (6.5)

8. Impractical and poor planning — better ego functioning in this area (6.5)

Work Patterns

I. Cessation of work when anxious for week or longer — shorter and lighter anxiety spells — depressions but no anxiety — works rather regularly (9)

II. Working out of a pantheistic feeling that stems from identification tendencies — working productively through identifications disappeared (7)

III. Compelled to withdraw to studio — studio visited out of free choice (7)

IV. Sense of guilt marks working — work without guilt (8)

V. Secrecy motivates work — other motivations primary (6.5)

VI. Artistic activity directly equated with "dirty" behavior — sense of derivative nature of work grows (9)

VII. Ego regression equated with insanity — no such equation (9)

VIII. Unable to integrate domestic life and creative work — integration of two domaines (2)

IX. Impractical in conduct of own affairs as teacher and producer of art — practical (5)

Discussion of Size and Distribution of Ratings

We note that at the completion of treatment it is still difficult for the artist to integrate domestic life (being wife, sweetheart, homemaker, and potential mother). In this respect no change was achieved, nor did the therapist actually attempt to attain much change, as was noted in the case report. It was felt that a change of balance in this direction would injure what for the patient had long been her primary focus in life, her creative work and preoccupation with art and music.

There is a marked change along Direction of Development VII from ego regression in creative work equated with insanity to a total acceptance of ego regression. This change enhanced the productivity of the patient enormously,and can be considered very important.

As far as anxiety interferring with the patient's work, we see that the aspired change is optimal, namely 9. The patient could work at any and all times that she desired, since she was freed entirely of the long anxiety attacks that had sent her restlessly pacing the streets, striving to allay anxiety by motoric activity. A third optimal change occurred with regard to the feelings that working creatively with clay and other moldable substances was a dirty activity to be kept secret and to censor.

We have, then, conspicuous forward movement along three highly important directions of development in the work area. Changes along the remaining directions in the work area are not optimal, but they can be considered incisive. Hence, again, as in the two previous cases, we may conclude that the work patterns were certainly not adversely affected by the treatment, which in this particular case probably saved the patient from a breakdown. Work was pursued as passionately as before treatment, and indeed several negative work habits improved notably. It must be noted that this artist had practically no problems that interfered with productivity per se except that evidenced in Direction of Development I which was completely overcome. The work patterns noted at the beginning do not reveal interferences with *productivity* but rather *the existence of pressures upon the artist's mood and feeling about herself* when she was at work. We can see that the depressants that existed were greatly reduced.

As far as dynamics of personality are concerned, there is an even more uniform picture of change. There is improvement along all the directions of development, with Direction III (withdrawal) showing less incisive change than is reflected in most other areas. In fact, the case report shows that the withdrawal from the environment was always paralleled by considerable artistic creativity. It appeared almost like a precondition for work and was so deeply ingrained in childhood and later trauma that it appeared doubtful whether complete alterations in this aspect could be effected.

Few of the ratings along the directions of development in personality are as high as those achieved in some of the other cases presented. The patient left treatment greatly helped, rescued from her anxiety, but with the imprints of the original problems visible.

It is clear that dynamics Direction 1 and work pattern Direction I are interrelated, for the cessation of anxiety led immediately to a tremendous upsurge in productivity.

Further connections between Direction of Development in Dynamics 2 and Direction of Development in Work Patterns II, between Direction of Development in Dynamics 3 and Direction of Development in Work Patterns III, Direction of Development in Dynamics 4 and Direction of Development in Work Patterns IV, Direction of Development in Dynamics 6 and Direction of Development in Work Patterns VI, and Direction of Development in Dynamics 8 and Direction of Development in Work Patterns IX are evident. Because of the similarity between the problem in the personality area and the problem in the work pattern area it is understandable that the increases in rating are similar in both areas, although the improvements in work patterns are almost always more clearly marked.

We deal here, then, with a case in which the improvement in personality is considerable though not total, and where the creative productivity and improvements in work patterns is very high. The only factor threatening work, namely anxiety, has been completely removed.

Changes of Work Patterns

Tina Mandell started to paint a very short time after she quit college, which she had attended for two years. At the time she entered treatment she had won two prizes and had shown her work in three important group shows. At the termination of treatment she had won several more prizes, was selling all the work she produced and had had several prominent shows.

When the patient entered treatment she considered her work of secondary importance to her marriage. When treatment was concluded her work had become of far greater importance and the artist was undecided which way to turn her energies, towards her work or the risking of a new marriage and creation of a family.

When this patient entered treatment she could not work at all during periods of anxiety. When treatment was terminated her anxiety was alleviated. Among the various factors causing anxiety, the following was most prominent. The patient, an excessively masochistic woman, invited injury at every turn. When she was actually hurt by another person her ensuing rage reactions took a special course. She turned the rage against herself, seeing herself as a loathsome, worthless individual. When this occurred she would feel that she was unattractive, incompetent, and odd. However, at this inversion another rage impulse was set off. It was directed at the very mechanism that had compelled her to turn the rage on herself rather than on the person who had injured her. She then lamented and resented the self-degradation her unconscious had brought about. She realized that her experiences were not realistic and yet only very slowly did she learn to emerge from them. This once more intensified her anger. Her control over these layers of anger was feeble, and her method of defense was to keep herself very active motorically, but inactive artistically. Hence there were long artistic lulls when anxiety set in. After she had learned to make contact with her rage, the turning against herself and the renewed anger at her self-induced humiliations, and had gained insight as well as enhanced control over these systems, the patient was invariably able to extricate herself from this cycle. Thus her anxiety was eliminated, and work interferences were entirely avoided.

Except for anxiety periods, she was never blocked. There existed no period whatsoever outside of the anxiety condition where ideas, inspiration, or impetus to create were inaccessible to her. Her spirit of invention was inexhaustible. She frequently worked twelve to fourteen hours at a stretch. Yet she had definite work problems of a different sort.

During the second and third years of treatment the artist, with a great deal of difficulty, disclosed and discussed her habit of drawing in a small, much-fingered notebook, designs which she said she had refrained from executing on canvas. The designs she showed the therapist appeared to be highly original and craftsmanlike; they represented exquisite basic themes and variations on these themes. They combined imagination with highly skilled execution. The reason for the patient's reluctance to discuss her designs, and what is more important, her hesitation to execute them, was her fear that the sketches disclosed what she considered an underlying madness. She equated freedom from defenses and control, that is, her own far-reaching ego regression when engaged in work, and the deviation of her sketches from routine, with madness. The therapist and the patient then discussed in detail the difference between sheer madness without content and ego regression in the service of creativity, resorting to illustrations from the lives and works of great artists. The mere articulation of the fears and the fact that the therapist had seen the designs which had previously embodied for the artist a nucleus of insane tendencies that she revealed to no one had an immediate salutory effect. This was unexpected by the therapist, and the speed with which change set in also was unexpected. The artist's relief seemed total, her comprehension of the distinction between insanity and regression seemed immediate and deep. Understanding brought about a marked change.

It must be added that this artist had often dwelled on connections felt to exist between painting and creating of collages, and urinary, excretory, masturbatory activities and other forms of play with "dirt" in youth and later life. It is most likely that the notion of insanity that attached to her sketches had considerable connection with guilt feelings over playing with "dirty things." She seemed to feel odd because of doing this, and expected to "go crazy" as punishment. Yet the immediate and lasting relief came as the direct consequence of initiating the therapist to the supposedly "mad" world of her sketches.

After two therapeutic hours of reviewing the differences between psychotic regression and regression that accompanies creative work, she permitted herself to convert her sketches into actual work. From that point on she completely lost all fear of her ideas. She accepted them, selected and organized them, and executed them many times. She occasionally mentioned thereafter that no design, no novel form, no invention or idea produced for the sake of creative work frightened her.

This young artist experienced a deep cleavage between her personal life and her work as an artist before and during treatment. This was true despite the fact that her husband, and subsequently a boy friend whom she loved deeply demanded almost no domesticity from her. When she was working at her studio she was invigorated, inspired, industrious, often in high spirits. As she left for home a sense of inner division took hold of her. She felt that she must leave the life of the artist behind and enter into another, that of a loving woman, neat, organized and attractive. At first she experienced the womanly phase of her life as demanding and full of pressures, which she recognized as coming largely from within herself. Though this improved greatly, she was not too well able to integrate the two aspects of her life. It was not easy for her to bridge the two domains.* Throughout treatment the patient made little progress in shifting smoothly from one area of functioning to the other. When she left treatment, with anxiety eliminated and the earlier paranoid thinking gone, she was gravitating toward making her personal life the nucleus of her existence. This direction was not felt consciously to be painful. Yet her dreams and other indices showed regrets and conflicts on an unconscious level. The life of the artist was of focal importance to her, and she often dreamed that she was ill as a symbol of feeling creatively deprived.

Tina's creative life had started in mid-adolescence when the latent rebellion against her loving but severe parents began to take concrete shape. Her rebellious spirit lead her away from the bourgeois existence of her parents into a world of books, art

---

*This problem has also been found in other female artists under treatment.

and music. She spent her days visiting museums and libraries, sketching in the park and collecting unusual records. At night she would smuggle herself, sketches and records into the house, avoiding any contact between her two worlds.

Secrecy continued to play an important part in the patient's creative experiences. She preferred to work alone. She never showed her sketches or unfinished pieces to anyone. Moreover, a sense of guilt attached to her work, left over from the fact of smuggling her possessions into her parent's home. During the first two years of treatment the compulsive need for secrecy changed little. She needed to be furtive in order to enjoy her work. Yet when she was furtive she felt guilty. One reflection of this was her preference for working late at night and into the early morning. These hours, she felt, were stolen hours, therefore better hours. As the connections became clearer between this need for secrecy and the rebellion against her parents, and as the hostility towards the parents gave way to affection, the need for secrecy diminished. It was replaced by a new experience in working alone; one of privacy and friendly isolation rather than secrecy. When this change of mood occurred, guilt also disappeared to a large extent, as reflected in the rating of eight along Direction of Development in Work Patterns IV.

As she worked through both the open hostility and the largely repressed hostile feelings toward her parents, Tina developed much tolerance and tenderness for them. She was able to enter their world without suspicion and a desire to withdraw. This also applied to the world in general. Where previously she had alternated between gentleness and warmth and pronounced hostility and withdrawal, she now became genuinely friendly and interested in others. Yet human contacts often played a secondary role. The essence of her life remained her art. Her own work, and the enjoyment of other artistic pursuits remained a solitary occupation, cut off from the concerns of day-to-day life.

The wounds of childhood never quite healed, and their remote scars were reflected in a gentle understanding of all human suffering and in her dedication to the world of art—that world that was most truly real to her.

Although she received acclaim early, the admiration and praise of others had no influence on her work attitudes. She worked well regardless of outside opinions and influences. The problem so often noted with creative persons—as shown so clearly, for example, in Case No. 5—that is, an inability to continue working once success has been achieved, never existed for Tina Mandell. Many artists who produce a work or series of works that obtain public acclaim, have difficulty in going on to new achievements. They feel compelled to top their previous performance; they become self-conscious on account of the acclaim; or they are torn between the desire to repeat or modify the successful work and the inner necessity to move along new directions. Untouched by acclaim, these conflicts were unknown to Tina.

CHAPTER 6

The Case of Lewis Nordlund, an Actor-Singer

Case Report

Lewis Nordlund entered treatment at twenty. He was an unmarried singer and actor who had achieved professional recognition and success in off-Broadway and Broadway plays, musicals and revues. When he applied to the Arts Project for intensive psychoanalytic psychotherapy, he had already been in treatment for four months with a private medical analyst, on a once-a-week basis. But because he felt that he needed more frequent sessions than the private fees permitted, he asked us for help.

On acceptance as a candidate for treatment, Lewis was assigned to a male therapist with whom he was in treatment three times a week for a period of over one year, after which time he asked for a transfer to another therapist. This time he was assigned to a female therapist. The details of this first therapeutic experience will be presented later, together with the reasons for his eventual transfer. The patient thereafter was in treatment for three years.

Lewis was a pleasant, slightly built, boyish-looking young man who emanated an attractive quality of naiveté, youth and surface bouyancy. He himself, as it soon turned out, was not sure about his personal attractiveness either with regard to looks or personality and questioned his appeal and his personal and creative caliber constantly. As far as appearance was concerned, the screening psychiatrist, as well as the two therapists in the Arts Project who worked with Lewis, were aware of a certain immaturity of appearance but felt that the patient had an appealing quality which he himself did not recognize and therefore did not see as a personal asset that could enhance his constantly fluctuating, generally negative self esteem. According to all the experts who saw this young man, he had the kind of presence that was appropriate for his theatrical career and that was reflected in a naive but appealing quality of appearance and speech.

The patient was direct and clear about his wish for therapeutic help. From the first session on, he reiterated his feelings of helplessness and dependency and pleaded for love on the part of the therapist. Attractive as he was, he could often be ingratiating in speech and manner. He suffered from frequent anxiety, masked by a studied poise and calm but discernible on occasion through restless and fidgety body movements, sweating forehead and palms, pleading and averted glances.

Lewis' presenting problems, as he stated them, were lack of confidence, feelings of immaturity, exaggerated preoccupation with himself and his own thoughts, and an unrealistic approach to life and people. He felt that he lacked control and discipline in all areas of life. His emotions shifted constantly and so did his thoughts. He could not rest with any topic to a degree where it could be perused and surveyed, not to mention analyzing and coming to grips with it. He had little discipline as far as furthering his career was concerned, and would not visit agents regularly. If he made contacts, he was not able to sustain and deepen them. His financial affairs were in disarray. He had many debts and spent money impulsively and imprudently. In his own words this was the situation: "My thinking and decisions have nothing to do with facts. I do not deal with what really is but with that I think it or wish it to be. My thoughts are the result of feelings which vary with different occasions. I lack control and discipline in all directions of my life. I want to break away from this little-boy pattern. My creative energies, which are substantial, are blocked because of my personal difficulties which create constant frictions and uncertainties."

The urgency and honesty with which the actor stated these problems, specifically his awareness of infantile dependent needs, the oral origin of which he understood and felt, and his strong desire for better ego functioning were considered therapeutic assets. We weighed thoroughly the pros and cons of admitting him into the project. Among the counterindications was his great ego weakness, especially his instability which outdistanced that of any other candidate who was accepted. Also, Lewis Nordlund appeared to be functioning on a lower level of artistic experience and accomplishment than all but the last candidate described in this report. However, his intense desire to help himself, and his evident theatrical talent were considered sufficient to accept him as a candidate whose progress would be interesting to study. It was obvious that he needed help urgently.

The specific difficulties which the patient experienced as a professional singer and actor were manifold and were stated and reiterated by him from the first session on. He had difficulty in contacting agents, and when he did he had trouble presenting himself and his qualifications realistically and to his best advantage. "I never know if the agents are truly interested in me. I feel that they are doing me a favor when they talk to me. Their approval becomes so important to me, that I get a helpless feeling. If agents contact me, I feel more confident."

During auditions, the patient generally became overwhelmed by strong feelings of competitiveness and inadequacy. "I compare myself with others, and don't come out on top. I can't relate to people. I get jealous and try to cover my feelings of hostility. I never feel that I am as good looking, talented or virile as others in my field. I am usually tense and present myself in an unfavorable light."

During rehearsals the patient never felt relaxed. He was too "other directed" to permit this. The focus was constantly on how *others* were reacting to him. This deflected from his spontaneity and freedom of expression. He was hampered in his ability to take cues and directions. "I don't feel free to experiment. I think of what someone else would do with this part or in this particular situation. Someone who I think is a better actor or a stronger person. I anticipate that people will not find me interesting. I feel that my talent is not as big as others."

The patient's difficulties with other actors were described as follows: "I'm jealous of them. I resent them if they get laughs. I resent their freedom at rehearsals. I'm jealous of the rapport which they have with the director."

He frequently had difficulty in creating a character he was portraying, and was anxious during performances. "If I do not have a strong feeling of acceptance from the audience, I find it difficult to be free. I can't be assertive in what I am doing. This need to please takes away from my performance."

His attitudes and reactions to audiences were as follows: "About the worst thing that can happen to me on stage is when I lose concentration, and put all my focus on the audience.. Then I have resentments, and I feel like a helpless child. I become immobile. I don't like to feel resentful to the audience, but this I find comes when I feel that they don't like me, or if their reactions are less enthusiastic than I had from a good audience the night before."

Asked about his feelings about being an actor, the patient's response was: "What I doubt more than my talent is my temperament. I'm afraid that I don't have enough ego strength. A primary thought I have is whether I really want the theater and am suited for it. I don't mean talent-wise. For all my doubts I believe that I can entertain—but I get nervous and frightened. I'm a hard type to cast commercially. I'm not a leading man. I'm not the usual juvenile, so I've got to believe in myself twice as much as the other guy because I'm selling a personality. I think of someone who is vivacious and charming. I'm not that, even though I try to be."

The patient's background and family history shed some light on the early influences shaping his attitudes and work difficulties. He was the youngest of three children, one of whom died at birth. His sister is four years his senior. His father, an antique dealer, died of tuberculosis when the patient was nineteen years old. Family life was characterized by continual friction between his parents, rivalry with his sister, and arguments with his father. He believed that his father favored his sister, while he was "mother's little boy." The father was described as a man with many prejudices and insecurities, a person who worked hard all his life but never enjoyed the fruits of his labor. With friends and acquaintances the father was affable, charming and well-liked. He sang, told jokes, was the life of the party, and fulfilled a great need for approval and recognition through these endeavors.

To the world his father presented a picture of strength which Lewis admired and ardently wanted to emulate. On another level, however, Lewis was aware that his father had deep feelings of insecurity and inadequacy which he chose to keep secret from others but which he expressed within the privacy of the family. "He would take it out on me, or my mother." He was critical and given to temper outbursts. Lewis perceived that his father resented the son's musical talents which were in evidence at an early age. Even before he was five, Lewis recalled that his mother encouraged him to dance and sing for guests. Lewis felt uneasy if his father was there at such times. He was certain that his father resented him. His evidence for this was a disapproving expression on his father's face. He believed that his father resented sharing the limelight and so was highly competitive with him. Lewis was always convinced that his success was his father's failure. Each time he contemplated a successful venture he was sure it was a hostile and destructive act against his father. This left him with a continual feeling of uneasiness and anxiety and he constantly anticipated his father's anger and disapproval. He was sure that his father resented him when he won the junior high school drama award, and was later picked as "the boy most likely to succeed."

The patient's entire family appeared to be musically endowed. His mother danced and sang, but did not have formal training. She had a good voice and sang continually while she did her household chores. Lewis' sister also sang and danced; his father was an excellent whistler. While the atmosphere in the home was expressive of a good deal of talent, it was also permeated by conflict and competitiveness. This has had a stifling effect upon Lewis' freedom of expression and personal security.

One might speculate at this point about the difference between talent and what we might call true creativity. Because the patient came from a family background where talent abounded, we might conjecture about the constitutional and hereditary factors inherent in this talent. Nonetheless, it is important to take into account the influence that the environmental and emotional factors in the patient's life had on the actual development and mode of expressing his musical gifts. In the treatment of this patient there was no doubt that he was a very talented individual, but some questions occurred from time to time to all those who knew the case about whether he could truly be considered a creative person.

He was the only one in the family who sought professional training and desired to make singing and acting his career. He felt that his mother tried to place obstacles in his way by continual scepticism about his chances of being successful. Despite her over-anxiety and over-protectiveness, Lewis felt that he had a better relationship with her than with his father. She was described by him as alternately weak and ineffectual and driving and controlling. She was given to sudden outbursts of anger, followed by seemingly seductive as well as infantilizing endearments.

Lewis believed that his mother sought to keep him in a totally dependent position, and to this day she treats him like an incompetent child. Up to the second year of treatment Lewis lived in his mother's small apartment, with his sister, her husband, and her little daughter. The mother repeatedly called Lewis by the sister's or the little granddaughter's name, which reflected the confusion and haziness of the family relations. Lewis' own self-image was one of being childish and inadequate and indicated his identification with his mother's image of him.

An early feminine identification was also evident in the patient's intense envy of his sister. Because he felt that she received more than he did, he grew up with the feeling that girls were better than boys. As a child, he played with the girls and pretended that he was one of them.

The patient's sexual identity, as can already be gathered, was not at all stabilized. Psycho-sexual development was impaired as he had been unable to resolve his strongly dependent and all-pervasive attachment to his mother. On the other hand, the frightening and unapproachable father figure seemed to have made a satisfactory male identification virtually impossible.

From a psychodynamic point of view, there was little doubt that the patient's difficulties in expressing the full potential of his talents were intricately bound up with intense competitive strivings with his father. It is interesting to note that while the father attempted to present a picture of strength to the outside world and to keep his weaknesses a secret, the opposite was characteristic of Lewis. To the outside world he attempted to present a picture of helplessness and inadequacy, while growth strivings and his innate abilities and strengths were kept a closely-guarded secret. This had been one of the most striking revelations in his Rorschach test. The patient's intellectual functioning was found to be in the superior range. Although this was so, his attitude toward his superior intellectual functioning seemed to be of a disdainful, depreciating nature, in the same way that he down-graded his masculinity, talents and other abilities. Self doubt, anxiety about self-assertive activity and strong repressive measures impoverished his intellectual activity. His major defense mechanisms to ward off unconscious conflict and anxiety were repression, obsessive doubting, projection and withdrawal from anxiety-provoking situations. Weak ego functioning and continual repression and projection of feelings accounted for Lewis' constricted, infantile behavior.

Why Lewis avoided successful strivings and overt expressions of aggression was understandable. These symbolized open competition with his father and the threat of personal injury. To behave like a self-assertive, potent man implied possession of a penis which could be harmed. Hence, self castration in the form of infantile, masochistic and self-defeating behavior appeared to be the lesser of two evils.

Lewis denied his masculinity quite openly. This denial occurred in sessions in which he repeatedly presented and identified himself as a helpless, asexual little boy. In public bathrooms he compulsively compared the size of his penis unfavorably with those of other men. In homosexual activity he usually assumed the passive feminine position. He rarely had an erect penis in sexual activity. His associations to his frequent indulgences in the practice of fellatio indicated a perception of fused sexuality in his partner. The penis was perceived by the patient as a breast, and he attempted frequently to recreate the nursing situation where he felt like the suckling infant. Feelings of great dependency, rivalry and rage existed in all of his homosexual relationships.

The patient could only be successful on a fantasy level, and only if this was in the image of a person other than himself. Ethel Merman and Cary Grant were his two idols, and he frequently imagined that he was one or the other. Because one person's success represented another person's failure in Lewis' perception, he reacted with extreme envy and rage each time a fellow actor or singer received recognition and praise. He behaved as if it were a personal deprivation or injury. Omnipotence permeated other fantasies. A repetitive fantasy was that he "would walk out on the stage, do nothing, and the audience would break into tremendous applause and shouts and this would go on for at least twenty minutes." His concept was that his very presence, rather than what he produced, was worthy of such acclaim.

The actor's relationships with men were summed up succinctly in the following statement, made by him. "I like to please men, to entertain them, but I would also like to stab them in the back." This undoubtedly characterized the nature of his transference reactions to his first therapist in the project.

The patient's anxiety and fear of the therapist was masked by passive and ingratiating behavior in therapy sessions, with attempts to please or placate the therapist and to look to him for complete solutions. Despite overt compliant behavior Lewis was basically rebellious and negativistic. He refused to make the small financial contribution to treatment expected of him as a token effort on his part and sabotaged therapy by long and protracted interruptions for out-of-town theater work. Because of negative transference and counter-transference reactions, the relationship between the patient and his male therapist was mutually terminated.

Because there appeared to be a stronger feeling of threat in relation to male figures, it appeared that the patient might work more comfortably with a woman therapist. Nonetheless, it was anticipated that his dependency upon, as well as his fear and hostility toward all authority figures would become manifest regardless of the sex of the therapist. This, of course, proved to be true.

From earliest contacts with the female therapist, Lewis behaved in the same disguised and ingratiating manner. He presented himself as weak and helpless, yet seemed subtly engaged in a struggle for power and control. He acted out his passive and infantile attitudes regarding nurturance and acceptance, and his major emphasis was on soliciting direction and reassurance. He denied the significance of his own attitudes and feelings and behaved in therapy as he did in other areas of his life, where his reliance upon the protectiveness of others tended to cancel his own judgments and self-assertion. With the patient's insistence upon presenting himself as weak, helpless and inadequate, it became clear through analysis of his transference attitudes that he was attempting to please the therapist in the same way he did his mother. He had always perceived her encouragement of his weakness and dependency upon her as a sign of love and protection. It was essential fairly early in treatment to interpret this transference attitude, and to clarify the true nature of the therapist's alliance with his strengths and capacities rather than with his neurosis. This had an immediately freeing effect upon Lewis, with ego-strengthening concomitants.

Therapy dealt with Lewis' underlying fear of his aggression and anger and his anxiety about punishment and rejection. This was done partly by analyzing his associations to his parents and his early life experience and was worked through within the transference relationship.

The patient's infantile strivings were identified and interpreted as a defense against underlying anxiety associated with success and self-assertion. Specific kinds of anxiety were focused on, relative to the patient's activities and verbal, as well as nonverbal, communications. Dreams and fantasies were an important therapeutic medium for eliciting associations about unconscious conflict and fear.

The patient's ambivalent feelings were recognized, identified and worked through. Verbal and emotional expression was encouraged and supported. Analysis was stressed in contra-distinction to destructive acting out behavior, such as exhibitionism and homosexual pick-ups which lowered his self-esteem and the long interruptions in the therapeutic relationship which prevented him from successfully resolving his problems.

Resistances were constantly worked through, and ego strengths and reality testing constantly supported. The therapist perceived Lewis as a frightened adult with strengths as well as weaknesses. This was contrary to the patient's neurotic need to be seen and related to as a helpless dependent child. The reality of his maleness and adulthood was constantly stressed, while unconscious conflict, fear and anxiety expressed through dreams and fantasies were analyzed.

Healthy goals and strivings were supported and encouraged, while self-defeating tendencies were explored and interpreted. This was particularly relevant and meaningful in relation to the actor's unconscious wish to use therapy masochistically and to turn it into another self-defeating experience.

Some of his intense transferences to authority figures were viewed in terms of early child-parent relationships. Reality perceptions were strengthened through the process of exploring the patient's projections onto authority figures, and by separating realistic threats and dangers from fantasies and anticipated hurts and rejections.

The patient's financial contribution to therapy was elevated commensurate to his realistically improved financial situation. This was ego strengthening, and reinforced the concept that he was viewed as an adult with the capacity to meet adult responsibilities, and that his success was based on his efforts and participation rather than on omnipotent magic. Lewis' motivation was increased, as well as his work capacity. Towards the end of treatment he was working regularly, earning a good income, and his neurotic passivity was definitely on the wane.

The male therapist who first treated this actor when he was accepted by the Arts Project had a good many counter-transference feelings towards this provocative and self-pitying patient who constantly and articulately demanded expressions of love and praise within the therapeutic situation. While patients often crave similar support from the therapist in a more indirect and often unconscious manner, this young man was very verbal about his demands, at the same time that his behavior, in a less direct fashion, was ingratiating. The impact of the patient's transference was so powerful that the male therapist on various occasions fell prey to his counter-transference feelings. He either allowed his compassion for Lewis to compel him to extend special support to Lewis or else permitted feelings of irritation over the ingratiating behavior of Lewis to color the therapeutic relationship. Lewis acted out his demands, many of which were quite conscious, in so forceful a way that the therapist was sucked in by them and also acted out his feelings. This is an interesting situation especially in view of the fact that the therapist, a highly experienced and capable man, never experienced similarly intense counter-transference feelings. This actor, like other actor patients who have been observed outside the Arts Project, demonstrated, as it were, his artistic potential and skill in the therapeutic situation. He was able to project his emotions so powerfully upon the therapist as to elicit uncommonly strong counter-transference reactions which showed in the therapist's facial expressions and behavior.

The second therapist who treated Lewis within the Arts Project profited from the experience of the first therapist. She made a special effort to be continually aware of counter-transference reactions both toward the patient's repetitive pleas for emotional support and toward his skillful provocations. She did not get involved in either an overprotective role such as the mother had played, or in a punitive, rejecting role such as both parents had taken in the past and into which the patient attempted to push the therapist with much aggressive energy and skill.

From the point of view of therapeutic technique it is important to mention that therapy in this, as in all the other cases, did not focus on the patient's creativity per se, even though Lewis seems to have discussed his work more often and at greater length than most of the other candidates in the project. Lewis Nordlund brought out many associations relevant to his work and repeatedly talked about work problems, such as his competitive feelings towards other actors, his reluctance to seek out agents and producers and his awkwardness whenever he was face to face with them. It was the therapist's plan to focus on the patient's personal functioning primarily and not to dwell too much on his work. It had become clear that the patient's work on stage and in rehearsal provided him with important channels for expression feelings and drives which in real life were blocked. This was true of nearly all feelings, as we shall see, aggressive and sexual. The drives were deflected from their original aims and channeled into roles on the stage. This represented undoubtedly a form of sublimation and is quite in line with Bychowski's idea (2) that in the artist sublimation processes are exceptionally broad in range and deep in intensity. There is no doubt that in this young actor the expression of emotion which took place on the stage in the form of theatrical roles prevented a more far-going deterioration of the personality. Disturbed though he was, he would have been much more impoverished without the theater. This was clearly demonstrated during periods when he was not acting. At such times all symptoms became intensified. It was considered important therefore, to keep the work area intact and to arouse as little anxiety as possible about expressing himself in work, while unconscious conflicts and anxieties were being worked through in relationships and areas not connected with the theater. This permitted Lewis to hold onto healthy defenses and to derive important ego-building satisfactions while therapy was in progress.

On the stage, the patient was and is able to satisfy his needs for nurturance and acceptance from others. He was placed in the position of acting out masculine and heterosexual roles which gave him a sense of mastery over the anxiety related to these roles in real life. In addition, the theater offered the opportunity to express feelings which he normally had great difficulty with, namely overt aggression and self-assertion. We see, thus, that the sublimation of aggressive drives which Sterba and Sterba (9) traced in the work of the great sculptor took place quite consciously in the work of our actor-singer. "If I couldn't act, I might want to hurt someone," he once said. The stage also provided Lewis with a means for expressing warm, friendly and loving feelings without the threat of a close and intimate relationship. In addition, and possibly more important, it permitted a positive and non-threatening identification with the aspects of his father's personality which he admired most— namely his ability to sing and to entertain people.

The participant therapists of the Arts Project, in trying to steer their patients towards greater emotional health, never took the position that the creative work, whether painting, sculpting, acting or writing, should be used as substitute functioning in those areas where the creative person had conflicts and showed ego weaknesses of various kinds in real life situations and relationships. We all did assume, though, that while the patient was barred by various neurotic manifestations from healthy expression, his creative pursuits should be safe-guarded. They should continue to provide him with safety valves for expressing what otherwise had to be repressed, and for permitting the ego to function at high levels. It was for instance expected that to the degree that Lewis Nordlund—as well as other patients—could be helped to work out and resolve his anxieties and conflicts to that degree he would at a later point have a freedom of choice. He could utilize the freed energies and the newly-acquired functions more extensively in his private life or continue concentrating on professional and creative work as the prime arena for staging the exciting pursuit of life. In other words, we assumed that prior to successful therapy the patient was *compelled* to express himself in the creative field, while during or after therapy he had a choice.

We were, of course, not sure when we started upon the project to what extent a creative person who seeks refuge in work as a safe field within which to express drives that otherwise had to be repressed, or held in check through other defenses, would continue to devote energy to the creative work, once it was no longer urgently needed as a "safe area" a "haven" where no punitive measures need be expected. Would someone restored in a certain area now take his or her energies into real life, or decide to divide them between real life and creative work? It is to this question that the data we collected are giving an answer. In the present case the patient not only lived better after therapy but also worked more intensely, with more direction and more external success, if this be used as one of the criteria of achievement.

Specific changes that took place first in Lewis' personality and then in creative work were multiple and all for the good. Lewis' relationship with his mother became a more mature one and he ceased to occupy the old dependent childlike position in relation to her. Instead of relying upon her for money to meet his expenses, he now supports himself very adequately. He moved away from home and shared an apartment with a friend. He severed a self-destructive sado-masochistic homosexual relationship which had existed for years. The patient began to date girls and had his first experiences in heterosexuality.

There were realistic and noticable changes in his work patterns. He became more assertive in establishing contacts with agents, won a scholarship to attend acting classes with a renowned studio. He no longer maintains an omnipotent and magical approach to success. He has become aware that his success in the theater requires study, practice and improvement in his theoretical and technical knowledge and approach. In his spare time he has directed young people in acting and produced a musical show at a neighborhood church. He discovered abilities he had never realized he possessed. His relationship with directors is on a more friendly and less negativistic basis. A spirit of friendly cooperation exists in his relationship with fellow actors, where once there was great envy, distrust and childish competition. All of these changes have provided ego rewards for the patient and are helpful in making possible his eventual goal of achieving success in the theater.

Predictions

Prediction #1

The patient suffers from what he calls "low energy." This condition, which clinically can be described as the subjective experience of a passive-dependent orientation, makes him lean on other people, theatrical agents, directors and other actors amongst them. Filled with low self esteem, to a large extent because of infantile orality and the described dependency, he cannot present himself and his qualifications realistically and impressively. *It is predicted that the patient will become more independent, that the passivity will give way to initiative and self-confidence. He will obtain more self esteem, present himself more favorably to agents and directors and find more steady employment.*

Results: *This prediction came true.*

Prediction #2

The patient is confused as to his psychosexual status. He has repressed his heterosexual feelings to large extent and looks defensively for homosexual contacts. His confused sexual identity contributes considerably to his low self esteem, since he senses himself to be a confused little boy and not a man. He feels that he fakes being a man and that people can see through this. *It is predicted that there might be some modification in this area and that the patient might obtain a more clearly and realistically defined sexual male identity.* However, one cannot predict just how much progress can be made as ego strength is very weak. The patient is not distracted in his work too much by the confused sexual identity since it is all right with him to "act out" male figures. Hence progress in his work is predicted only in the sense that, more sure of his sexual identity, the patient will contact agents and directors more confidently.

Results: *Progress was more decisive than the prediction forecast. The patient was able to free his heterosexual feelings to some degree, to establish some contacts with females, and his confidence in negotiating with agents and directors improved markedly.*

Prediction #3

The patient can only function when praise is clearly given him and when he is thus assured that he is accepted. This makes his contacts with other people very difficult. He is provocative to cover up his diffidence, or else awkward and anxious both off stage and on. *It is predicted that the patient will have more access to his own feelings when repressions are lifted and that he will not need to refer so much to what others think of him. Also, when he works through the transference feelings to authorities he will be less dependent on and less concerned with the appraisal that others give him. A substantial progress is predicted.*

Results: *This prediction came true almost to the degree here stated. The patient's other directedness diminished substantially.*

Prediction #4

The patient is extremely competitive and defends himself against these competitive strivings by masochistic, self-failing behavior. Naturally all this handicaps his creative capacities. He either expresses his competitiveness and hogs the stage whereafter he is intensely anxious about the wrath he incurred, or worse still, he holds himself back by defending himself against the competitive strivings. He then becomes humble and constricted. *It is predicted that the patient will be able to be considerably more assertive without feeling as intensely hostile as he now does. He will cease to fear retribution, and will abandon the masochistic defenses.*

Results: *The prediction was too optimistic. The patient did indeed improve but not to the degree envisaged.*

Prediction #5

The patient is often anxious, quivers inside and perspires profusely. Anxiety befalls him mostly when he is off the stage but occasionally when he is acting. It is difficult to tell to what degree the anxiety will subside, but *a reasonable degree of freedom from anxiety is expected.*

Results: *The patient was occasionally anxious at the time he left treatment, but in general the level and intensity of anxiety fell more than the above prediction foretold.*

Prediction #6

The patient's thoughts are disorganized. He has little control over his external affairs, such as financial and professional-artistic matters. This is a serious ego defect. *It is likely that this weak ego condition will remain in considerable degree.*

Results: *The patient improved somewhat beyond the degree predicted.*

Directions of Development and Ratings

Dynamics	*Work Patterns*
1. Reiterations of oral dependency	I. Creative work is a need — not

— unsuccessful attempts to find oral-dependent gratifications in transference — gradual use of adult ego — relatively mature object relations (7)

2. Masochistic using of own helplessness and passivity — insight into mother transference — no change in masochistic pattern — gradual changes — healthy assertiveness (7)
3. Low self esteem — paranoid expectations of ridicule — working through of many infantile strivings — growing self respect (7)
4. Fear of authority figures — realistic appraisal (7)

5. Denial of masculinity — insight into repressed oedipal feelings and nature of reaction formations — release of competitive striving towards men—masculine identity (5)

6. Homosexual feelings and contacts — fear of assertive women lessens — some heterosexual contacts — bisexuality (5)
7. Withdrawal of affect — overtly hostile expressions in transference — freeing of affect (6.5)
8. Other-directed (patient obsessed with concern about other people's opinions) — heightening of other-directedness — g r o w i n g sense of identity not through acting but through awareness of own feelings — growing self-directedness (5)
9. Slight depersonalization experienced as inner hollowness — sense of self through work —

a vocation — lack of identity compels actor to obtain sense of self through acting — lifting of repressions, growing awareness of strivings and true affect — creative work ceases to fulfilll the original function of supplying identity (5)
II. Great reluctance to contact agents and little work — several successful contacts — contacts agents more readily (7)

III. Presents himself diffidently and unrealistically to agents and producers — presents himself confidently (7)
IV. Anxiety during auditions and performance — anxiety free (4.5)
V. Self-defeating patterns — connections understood between these patterns and underlying competitive and omnipotent strivings towards other actors — connections with competitiveness towards father—emerging openly hostile conduct — gradual cooperation (5)
VI. Fear of audience — lesser fear with lessening of other-directedness (4)

sense of self through contact
with own emotions   (7)
10. Diffuse ego organization and
poor control — control in financial area only — better ego organization — better all around
functioning.   (3.5)

Discussion of Size and Distribution of Ratings

We see that there has been a forward movement in all areas, both as far as personality development and the work patterns are concerned. Interestingly enough, however, the improvements in personality appear more marked than those in the area of creative work. The patient, as a scanning of the rating readily shows, became quite decidedly a more mature and happier person. His career as an actor-singer improved since he became more confident in his contacts with agents and directors. Self-defeating repression of omnipotent and hostile striving was lifted in some measure and the patient became more direct and his emotional register more ready to be tapped in acting. Yet the improvements in the work area, according to the ratings, are not better than moderate. Lewis Nordlund became decidedly a better functioning person but remained moderately function-ing as an actor-singer.

The decisive changes which occurred in work patterns are reflected in Directions of Development in Work Patterns II and III. Lewis obtained a growing ability to function as an executive and administrative person, and could look for work, obtain work and carry it through. Self-depreciation, a prime factor in keeping this actor inactive for sustained periods, diminished greatly, and at the end of treatment he was continuously busy, a considerable accomplishment in therapeutic terms to be sure. On the other hand, anxiety—another prime reason for holding the patient's creative work back—diminished somewhat but did not disappear markedly.

One might say that opportunities for working multiplied. Avenues previously closed to this patient because of his neurotic anxiety, lack of self esteem and provocativeness which always alternated with self-degradation, now opened up. He secured considerably more occasions for expressing himself creatively. The performances themselves—the creative activity—changed. We see among the Directions of Development in Work Patterns not a single one that addresses itself to the quality aspect of the creative side. This is so because the quality of the acting rarely came under discussion, nor was this touched on in the realm of associations or dreams. Here was a person for whom the creative processes per se and the creative products were of secondary importance. The prime emphasis was on the "rescue functions" which the creative activities played. They served as props for the patient's arrested and conflict-ridden personality. The acting and singing had functions similar to those of neurotic defenses and mechanisms which protect and uphold the personality in its struggle with its own arrested condition. It is to the credit of both patient and therapist that when the personality became more mature and the ego somewhat strengthened work continued to be pursued more actively even though it no longer served to defend the patient against his conflicts.

In the area of personality development the ratings show that this young man made somewhat better progress in those areas that have to do with pregenital functioning—especially his passivity and masochism—than in directly genital functioning. This is indicated by ratings of 7 in Directions of Development in Dynamics 1, 2, 3 and 4, while Directions of Development in Dynamics 5 and 6, which reflect the genital level, have ratings of 5. As far as affect restriction is concerned the rating of 6.5 shows that this patient's improvement is similar to improvement in the other cases whom we are discussing: there is a freeing of affect but it reaches only a middle-of-the-road position. We are dealing here with an area where progress is both slow and partial, in this as in the other cases. It is noteworthy that this actor, who on stage was exhibitionistic, and in private life on occasion both exhibitionistic and voyeuristic, did not become free to draw on his affect, but at the end of treatment suffered from repression of affect as much as several of our other artists who are engaged in fields that make lesser demand on direct demonstration of affect than does acting.

We see that the patient remained "other-directed" to a considerable degree, as reflected by the rating of 5 in Dynamic Direction of Development 8. This relatively high degree of other directedness was not intended. The therapist, in consultation with the supervisory research staff and the other therapists, decided to touch on this area as frequently and firmly as possible. We all felt that the patient could only gain by being less concerned with the opinions of other people, even though this would deprive him of one of the motivations for acting, namely his enormous desire for praise. We expected that he would be on firmer ground if he were motivated more directly by his own inner promptings and emotions. He did not need, we decided, the circuitous route of acting in order to secure continuous praise from others. By being less preoccupied with other people's opinions he would be less selfconscious. We took quite a plunge in this regard, since we certainly did not wish to weaken the artist's motivations and were not totally sure how this man would proceed were he less other-directed. As Directions of Development in Work Patterns II and III show, both therapist and staff were vindicated since the patient, with other-directedness somewhat reduced, obtained more work, and worked better rather than less well. Heightened self esteem, reflected by a rating of 7 in Direction of Development in Dynamics 3, helped him. The drop in other-directedness, which was moderate because of the tenacity of the pattern, not because of feeble therapeutic intervention, did not detract from Lewis Nordlund's readiness and eagerness to seek and perform work. The actor, as we see, did not engage in acting and singing solely out of the wish to become desirable to an enthralled and loving audience. Other motivations were at work as well.

In conclusion it should be noted that improvement in all areas was gradual and slow. Owing to the poorly functioning ego which, as Direction of Development in Dynamics 10 shows, did not improve markedly, the patient constantly grappled with anxieties of disintegration. Each bit of progress was the result of hard work on the part of the patient and therapist.

Changes of Work Patterns

Because Lewis Nordlund dwelled so extensively in therapy on his work and many of his work habits, the patient's patterns in this area have been reviewed at length both in the case report and in the discussion of inter-connections between the Directions of Development in Dynamics and in Work Patterns, so we shall review the changes of work patterns only briefly.

When Lewis entered treatment he worked only intermittently, and was constantly in financial straits. The main reason for his erratic work situation was the fact that he did not dare to go out on auditions. He did not go after work and was not sufficiently well-known for agents and directors to go after him. His frequent fits of anxiety, his low regard for his capacities as an actor, and his awkward ways of introducing and delivering himself in auditions were the prime reasons for his desire to stay away from the contest which an audition represented. He preferred to remain in the secure, confining and at the same time hated restrictions of home with mother, sister and in-laws, or to spend time in rather loose relationships with friends.

The patient described this state in one of his answers to the first questionnaire submitted to him. He said: "I don't try anywhere near the extent that I should in contacting agents . . . During the meetings with an agent I don't feel relaxed. While I think I am an unusual type, I tell the agent I am too short or too stocky. I concentrate so hard on what the agent might think and on all the negative things he probably has in mind that I don't come out the colorful personality that I can be at times."

The artist's conduct in this area changed considerably because he gradually learned to be much more aware of the assets he possessed, in particular a sunny, often endearing personality. He contacted agents regularly at the end of treatment and was always working in one capacity or other. If he was not in a play or musical, then he would be busily and fruitfully engaged in other activities: he directed plays in a settlement house, started to write a musical review or worked in a music store where he was well paid and where his knowledge of music was an asset that assured him of work.

Connected with the periodicity of work at the beginning of treatment was, of course, financial insecurity. This was intensified by Lewis' inability to budget money and control spending sprees. In this respect a total change occurred. After two and a half years of treatment Lewis worked more or less steadily in the capacities described above, and towards the end of the third year of therapy he was always occupied, enjoyed his work more, and was financially secure. Financial security was not due as much to an increased discipline in spending as to the fact that his income became regular and increased considerably.

At the beginning of treatment the actor focused attention in a pathological way on other people, on agents, directors, other members of the cast, and on the audience for whom he performed. The condition was so accentuated that it hampered his work tremendously. To go back to his own statements, also in the first questionnaire, he said: "Because I am so preoccupied with everyone else, I am not free to experiment . . . Sometimes I rush my speeches to get them over with because I think that the people around or before me won't find me interesting enough. I must have a feeling of acceptance from the audience, or it is difficult to be free and exclude a sense of power about myself. I know that is going about it the contrary way. I've got to project that feeling of power so that the admiration comes back to me from the audience. It has to start from me. I must like that dependence, at least at some points, if I am to be a first-rate actor."

These feelings of reference, which at times had a paranoid cast, were modified somewhat during treatment, after they had at first increased. During the first ten months of therapy which Lewis spent with his male therapist he was intensely preoccupied with the therapist's critical feelings towards him, which were in part imagined and in part true because of the strong counter-transference. When he was transferred to a female therapist who focused on his masochistic self-depreciation, the preoccupation with the therapist's opinion of the patient and with other persons' concern with him diminished slowly. The patient reported occasionally that he felt free to concentrate on his own emotions and strivings rather than having to busy himself with what others might think of him. For instance, after a short tour abroad with a company that performed a musical comedy, he reported that he had a great deal of success. "I played on the instrument of my emotions," he told the therapist. "I was not compelled to be split down the middle and worry what other people thought. I had fun just doing my part. I have never been that good." Such self-directedness, which made Lewis a much better actor and singer, occurred from time to time, but could never be relied on, so deeply imbedded was the actor's preoccupation with what others might think of him.

When Lewis first came to treatment he largely repressed his omnipotent strivings. His dreams indicated that he wanted to be a king, a fairy prince, and among other actors the shining and sole star. His habit of berating himself, in part the outgrowth of the inadequate psychosexual and ego development that made him feel unsafe, inadequate and childlike, was on the other hand a defense against his omnipotent ideas that he was *the* greatest actor. Intensely jealous of other members in the cast and accustomed from childhood to outshine his father as an entertaining person in the family, where everyone was clowning, singing, and entertaining, he actually wished no one to shine except himself. Sensing the possible retributions which such ambitious feelings on his part would conjure up in others, he defended himself against his omnipotence by a humility that alternated with the much more fundamental cocky and provocative behavior. When Lewis felt humble, defended against omnipotent strivings and therefore relatively safe from the expected hostility of those around him, he was not free. His performances, though usually quite acceptable, suffered from this lack of inner freedom. He felt tied, he felt that his emotional range was limited, and he felt deprived of an inner force that was his during the more cocky, openly jealous and grandiose episodes. Interestingly enough whenever he was cocky and emotionally free he felt like a "boy," but when he was inwardly defended against grandiosity and more staid he had some inkling of his adult status. The pattern which was just described changed most conspicuously when Lewis was out of the country with the touring company. When physically away from the parental home and the therapeutic situation he was best able to utilize the insights he had gained in treatment. He was able, during that eight-week period of touring with the musical comedy cast, to shelve his omnipotent strivings in some measure and so the self-defeating restricting defenses against them could be abandoned. "I was cocky," he said, "but in a likable way. Everyone asked me out for drinks and the invitations started to come around the middle of the day, when I could barely open my eyes yet. I was great and I felt like a good person." However, such periods of behavior and acting, unfettered by the defenses that were set up against the basic envy, hostility and omnipotence, remained sporadic, though their incidence increased durnig treatment. Even in the last questionnaire Lewis stated, in answer to the question about how he felt toward other actors: "It is not my talent that I really doubt, in comparison with others. It is still my temperament. I am afraid that I might smash someone, hog all the scenes, take them away from the others without either really intending to be just that ambitious and without having the strength to withstand the crucifixions they would give me."

Lewis Nordlund possessed little ego strength when he entered treatment, which was why we hesitated to take him on. We finally decided to treat him in the Arts Project because it would be interesting to note how far such a bright, young and appealing person might get after ridding himself of conflicts and developing more ego strength. When he came to us he not only possessed few resources with which to withstand criticism and attacks, he also had little capacity for planning, for concentrating on his work and for disciplining himself in looking for work and sticking to it. As far as discipline was concerned we have noted that he improved greatly in several ways. For as we have seen he pursued working opportunities and stuck to his work conscientiously by the time he left treatment. But his powers of concentration, his ability to pursue clearly a certain path of thinking, and to stick to certain topics remained limited. A restless, sporadic quality remained and colored everything he said, thought or did.

Therapy was terminated by the patient rather abruptly. There were still many unresolved conflicts, but the patient was prepared to manage on his own.

Three years later, the patient contacted the therapist and advised that he had consolidated many of the insights which he had gained through treatment. He was successful in his work, had improved his acting and singing abilities and was achieving positive recognition of his abilities from critics, agents and the press. He was more confident in all of his interpersonal relationships—personally as well as professionally and described a happier, healthier approach to life and in his role as an entertainer. Lewis Nordlund admitted that without psychotherapy, these achievements would not have been possible.

CHAPTER 7

The Case of Samuel Ellington, a Writer

Case Report

SAMUEL ELLINGTON, a talented young writer, made some significant changes in his writing as development took place in his emotional life as a result of psychoanalytic psychotherapy. The changes indicate the way in which the artist, his work, and his dynamics are intertwined. This report will focus on the relationship to his mother, changes in his relationships with women, and the impact these had on his writing.

Sam started writing in high school, and by the time he was eighteen was already selling short stories. He seemed to have a gift for satire, and at the beginning of treatment was writing sophisticated stories for magazines. He wrote easily, had well-established work habits, and considered his work the one area of his life where he functioned well. However, he sought out help because he was increasingly disturbed by his inability to form enduring and meaningful sex relationships with anyone, finding sexual release only in the most transient homosexual contacts. His sense of urgency and his gift for writing are indicated in the following quotation from an early statement:

"I'm afraid that as I am now I will never be able to have a decent, and anywhere near stable love relationship with anyone, male or female. And I know, without that kind of relationship, or at least the valid hope for one, I will not be able to survive, either as a person or artist. I find myself unable to break habits which annihilate rather than increase the possibilities of this kind of desired relationship. While I insist that I want to be a lover and to be loved, I pursue in the homosexual world, the patterns which in the heterosexual world would be associated with a whore rather than a lover. In other words, the most transient, the one-night kind of relationships, which I now embark on without even the hope that they might develop into anything more.

"Until recently I felt that I had no complaint about being 'gay.' Lately it becomes undeniable to me that I've got plenty of complaints. I suspect that I'm so hostile to my own homosexuality that I won't even begin to admit to myself that I don't like it. I find myself crying out to be a lover and unable to move in any direction. All the sick defenses that I find in the 'gay' world rebuff me, and though I tell myself it is my world and I'm enjoying it, I am so obviously seeking only the most frantic kind of physical release in the chance of a casual pick-up, that I find it hard to believe my own lies any more. I'm beginning to suspect that I want to be a husband and a father, or at least a heterosexual lover, but that I'm afraid to take one small step in that direction on my own."

We see in Sam's background an almost classic picture of homosexual development. We find a weak father, an older brother with whom he could not compete, and rejection at an early age by an ambivalent, over-protective and seductive mother. Sam summed up his feeling in the bitter statement, "The last time my mother and father loved each other was the night my brother was conceived." His brother was three years older. His father was weak and unassertive, alternating between periods of steady employment and bouts of drinking that jeopardized the security of the family. Sam had strong memories of periods when his father had to leave home because of his escapades. After a time he would come back, beg forgiveness and then start the cycle all over again. On numerous occasions Sam would plead with his mother not to take the father back. The mother's attitude was that of a myrtyr. When the father came back he was kept an outcast on the fringes of the family. The mother constantly derrogated the father to Sam, confiding all her troubles to the boy, exhorting him not to be like his father. As a young child he was allowed to sleep in the parents' bed when the father was away. When he was six months old his mother took a job and continued to work throughout his childhood.

The patient felt some superiority over his brother since he

considered himself the mother's favorite. But inwardly he felt great anxiety that he might lose this position if he did not please her and obey her, and if he showed any signs of masculinity. This uneasy position was also frightening because of his mother's seductive behavior toward him. She would initiate "loving hours" where there would be mutual hugging and kissing. He became preoccupied with sex at an early age but was desperately afraid his mother would see an erection or some other sign of sexuality. He was afraid of his mother's inadequate controls and the wrath of his father and brother if they discovered his unconscious satisfaction. His later terror of women as engulfing and overpowering sexually reflects this early anxiety. He had always had women friends but related to them as if he were another woman. His sexual anxiety showed in the following dream after his first intercourse with a woman:

> "I am copulating with E. My penis is erect in her but I am held as in a vise. She was kind and nice to me before, but she has changed completely. She has a cruel, gleeful expression on her face."

The patient acted this out over and over in the transference with the therapist. At times his panic was so great that the therapist would perform fellatio on him that he would sit up from the couch and continue the session with his back to her, often looking around to be reassured by the expression on her face. He was a thumb sucker to quite a late age, and there was a struggle between him and his mother as she tried to stop this. He expressed his castration anxiety as he cried out one day, "She already had my penis, couldn't she at least let me keep my thumb!"

The profound feelings of unworthiness brought about by these early experiences caused him to develop compensatory feelings of grandiosity and omnipotence, a wish for control and power he sought later as a writer. Sensing no behavioral limits in the women around him, he had to manufacture his own. These were unnecessarily harsh and elaborate. He denied or distorted his own needs so that they were unrecognizable even to himself. He impressed everyone as being a warm, related person but he never felt close to anyone. He felt personally responsible for making his mother's life happy, as though he were the cause of her tragedy. He served, but all the time he felt he was being used. We see this pattern carried over later into all his relationships and into his sex life, where he fantasied himself a "whore."

Although Sam was productive and already enjoyed success in his writing, as treatment progressed we began to see the handicaps he had as a result of his internal problems. He allowed himself little satisfaction from his accomplishment, feeling it was only one more crisis he had passed when he managed to fool everyone. He constantly compared himself to others, was either superior or inferior, never equal. He was terrified of exposure in his writing, first of his homosexuality, and on a deeper level, of sexuality for women. He used his writings to distract others away from himself instead of expressing himself. Therefore, his work tended to be superficial, his writings mostly entertaining and funny, his characters satirical and unreal. He saw himself "prostituting" his art, as he did his life, by writing to please others or to make easy money. He was unable to back up his artistic production with conviction, was fawning and placating with publishers and editors, allowing them to change and distort his meaning without protest. Most dramatic of all, he wrote almost entirely from the standpoint of the woman. His stories almost never placed the man in the dominant position, so that the reader would know how he felt or what he saw.

He obtained specific satisfactions from his writing. Through it he could live vicariously and feel power over his difficulties. Through it he could experience all the virtues he longed for in relationships and express his anger against the figures he envied or disliked.

Having to deny his own identity because of the many dangers of being a person in his own right, in childhood he had little freedom except in his fantasy life. He spent long hours by himself playing out fantasy roles, mostly of women. He was very much afraid of being discovered, especially by his father, as though his father could see through the deception and punish him as the usurper.

A good part of his childhood was spent in a suburban community of families in a higher income bracket than his family.

In school he felt left out because he was not good at athletics like his brother. He set out to excel in grades and accomplishment, acting in school plays, editing the school paper, writing stories and plays.

In the beginning his dreams of success were measured in monetary terms. He imagined himself a famous writer, making a lot of money and impressing everyone. All of this would please his mother in the fantasy, but he would then have a strong impulse to spoil it for her by telling her he was a homosexual.

It would seem that the sense of power he recalled from his childhood, where everyone was there to serve him, was a wish rather than a reality, and that only in his writing was he supreme. It is noteworthy that he felt his talent was magical and "God-given." Thus he was allowed to exercise such power, but there was always the danger that in some magical way it could be taken away if the gods were displeased. In line with this thinking, he felt called upon to pay a high price for this gift. He had to relinquish all personal happiness, to choose between love and success. He could not believe one could have both, and suspected something was wrong when it happened. One friend, successful as an artist, was married and had a child. Sam sneered at this and speculated that his friend was really a homosexual underneath. He was able later in his treatment to relate this to his feeling that his mother gave up all personal happiness for him. After this he became interested in the lives of well-known artists who were homosexual but who through analysis were able to become heterosexual.

Sam also had the fear, mentioned earlier, that his talent might be rooted in childhood unhappiness and that if he got well he would no longer be able to create. His real fear, however, was of punishment. A powerful parent would deprive him of his forbidden fantasy life were it revealed.

As he began to change as a person he used his writing to help him work out and resolve his conflicts. When he was going through a period of terrible hostility to his mother he wrote a story about a young couple who were engaged in a struggle with the girl's mother, "a terrible bitch." He identified with the girl and was thus able to vent his wrath against his own mother in the story. When it was finished he did not like the ending and decided to rewrite it so that the reader would have compassion for the mother. This came with a partial resolution of some of his feelings about his own mother. For at that moment he had forgiven her.

Since Sam's life was so immersed in literature and reading, his own associations were to the writings of other artists who could express in their writing feelings he was experiencing. He was very preoccupied with the "Tea and Sympathy" theme, the Sherwood Anderson play about the relationship of a young boy and an older woman. Between the two times he saw the play there was a dramatic shift in his attitude. The first time, he saw the woman as only evil, using the boy for her own purposes, hurting and destroying him. The second time, he felt the warmth and compassion of the woman for the boy. Simultaneously with this came the recognition, "a mother stands between me and a young girl." He identified very much with Lillian Roth as she struggled with alcohol in her autobiography, *I'll Cry Tomorrow*, and with the tragic personal life of Judy Garland. His fear of his own destructiveness came out as he recalled the story, *Devil in the Flesh*, in which a young boy has a sexual relationship with an older woman who dies giving birth to his child.

As treatment progressed, Sam began to be more selective about the kind of stories he would write. He withdrew a story from a magazine because the editor had suggested changes which he felt destroyed the meaning of his work. He wanted to write more profoundly, but even here the demand on himself was not so great. He questioned, "Why does it have to be the greatest? If it's not Oedipus Rex I lacerate myself."

A very important crisis occurred when he had been in treatment about two years, producing marked changes in him both as a person and as a writer. Although he had always been productive, even during some rather anxious periods, he suddenly was unable to write at all. Instead, whenever he sat down at the typewriter he was preoccupied with sexual fantasies and a strong desire to masturbate. There followed a great flood of dreams, memories and violent expressions of feeling during his sessions. At this time the feelings about his mother reached their peak:

"Sex is a big phony expression of love. Love is a big trap, a locking effect, a sex machine. It castrates you ultimately. I established myself as a homosexual so that I would not have to have sex with a troubled and unhappy woman. As an adult I can tell all women I can't satisfy them. It seems like the labor of Hercules. I lost the right to my sexual desire for them. I'd fail."

It became evident to him why he needed to distort and displace his sexual feelings. Belatedly he began to develop great curiosity about sex, examined all the misconceptions he had; the confusion between genital and anal activities, his assumption that the man inflicts pain on a woman during intercourse. He was able to examine some of his toilet habits in this new light. He had previously needed to urinate and move his bowels too frequently, putting his penis down into the bowl as he sat on it. His fantasy of acting out intercourse with his mother became conscious along with the reasons for the anxiety he had always had, that there was an animal in the bowl that would bite off his penis. He sums this feeling up well in a song he found himself singing one day coming to a session:

"Every time my heart begins to dance
The world steps on my little toes
Every time I take a chance
I pay through my little nose."

It ends: "Leaving just a lonely little lady in the dark."

Shortly after this Sam was able to have intercourse for the first time with a woman, a girl he had been dating for some time and with whom he had a meaningful relationship. Soon after this he resumed writing, but with a difference. For the first time he became interested in the character of the man in the story. Starting out with the male character as weak, ineffectual, married to a jealous controlling woman, he took him through a process of gradual maturing. When the story was finished he felt satisfied that this was the kind of man with whom he could identify. He felt that the man was himself, and worried for a time about exposure. He expressed concern that "people would think only a screaming faggott could write that story." By this time he was less concerned about this and found support in the works of artists in the past. He could finally reveal to the world that he knew what a man felt like. He was a man.

Shortly after this he turned down a chance to write a novel because he did not feel it would be a best-seller. As his feelings about this were examined he brought out a childhood memory when he had to expose his genitals as a kind of neighborhood initiation. He had very vivid memories of the other children's expressions of scorn at their small size. Here we see again the relationship of his emotional problem to his work. Having a sure thing like a best-seller would prevent anticipated humiliation.

In the last six months of treatment Sam wrote a novel about the relationship between two people who, in spite of many struggles, are finally able to build something together. He did not lose his light touch, but it was woven into the serious threads of the relationship. In this story he not only expressed a hopefulness about himself, but finally in his own mind there began a reconciliation between his father and mother. He says:

> "In spite of my homosexual problem, somewhere in the nether regions of my lost youth, I have a very strong awareness of how I feel a man and a woman can have a good and happy life together."

In the following statements Sam has written a summary of this report that cannot be improved upon:

> "There is no question about it that when I was fourteen and decided to become a writer part of the inducement was that it would give me Identity. In my typically sleepy home-town writers *had* IDENTITY. But the fact that I *am* a writer leads me to believe that if I'd grown up in Keokuk I still would have been one. The desire to please Mumsie and the desire for identity were simply dead weight I carried along with me."
>
> "Lately it seems to me that there have been a lot more times when it was awfully hard for me to sit down at the typewriter and write. I don't know precisely what the reasons are. I guess for one thing discovering that part of my motives were to please mother and realizing that this kind of pleasing mother just can't be done in this world made it seem a little less important. Or maybe I wanted to get back at her by *not* having my name on that cover. The realization that it doesn't

matter to her one way or the other, it's happening to *me*, not to her, is the beginning of liberation."

"I'm beginning to become aware of the worth of my own feelings. Talent is the ability to articulate and express these feelings effectively. But if you don't trust in the feelings to begin with, or if you can't find them, you're dead from the start and you might as well write perfume copy."

Predictions

Prediction #1

This patient's personality is a very complex defensive structure evolved in response to the abandoning, unloving, threatening and devouring mother. It is probable that as he differentiates between the mother and other figures, both male and female, his partly hostile, partly witty defensiveness, now used to protect him against abandonment, will be modified. *Whether this will influence his work is impossible to say, but it will change his relations with agents, editors, and colleagues. His relations with them and with others will achieve more continuity. At present he gets along rather well, but only because he is able to sense his rising hostility and to cut short his relations.*
Results: *This prediction came true.*

Prediction #2

The patient has much contempt for himself, and obtains his primary sense of importance through his work. This is a major motivating force behind his driving himself to write on a compusively rigid schedule. *However, should this drive for esteem through his work diminish, he will not lack other motivations for writing. His preoccupation with ideas and the pleasure of words will always be a motivating force.*
Results: *This prediction proved true.*

Prediction #3

Sexual problems play a major role in the personality and are rooted in the relationship to the mother. *When the patient achieves a better understanding of this relationship, major personality changes will ensue. It is impossible to predict in what way this will affect work patterns, but it may be said that generally changes in work patterns are inevitable when such major developments in dynamics occur.*

Results: This prediction, although somewhat vague, proved generally correct. The patient gradually became capable of deeper relations, especially with one woman, and the manner in which male characters were treated in writing changed shortly thereafter.

Prediction #4

The patient will change very slowly. It is likely, therefore, that the change in work patterns will be slight.

Results: The development proved better than anticipated. The patient did change slowly indeed, but in general the work patterns changed more deeply than the dynamics.

Directions of Development and Ratings

Dynamics

1. Fear of abandonment — defends against it with hostility — tangential relations with others, always protecting against abandonment — abandoning others — abandoning less abrupt — no fear of abandonment   (4)
2. Need to control others — abandoning others as means of control — seeing control as defense — uses other defenses more often — need not control others   (4)
3. Wit, satire, and defensive hostility chief ways of relating — wit, satire, defensive hostility among many ways of relating   (5)
4. Self-contempt alternating with omnipotence — less self-contempt — less omnipotence — higher and more stable self-esteem   (5)
5. Rigidity and isolation of affect — affect released   (4)

6. Unaware of own needs, except

Work Patterns

I. Only writes when assured of status and money — selfcontempt because of this motivation — writes for many reasons, including wish to obtain status and money   (6)
II. Compulsive work schedule — flings (sometimes over a week long) to break away from schedule — greater flexibility   (6)
III. Writes only slick material — considers but hesitates to undertake meaningful assignments — more meaningful assignments — many meaningful assignments   (6)
IV. Routine writing (e.g., copying from earlier works — passionate writing   (7)
V. Focus on female characters — begins to become familiar with "feeling male" — focuses on male and female   (5)
VI. Insists on suffering as pre-

oral and anal — growing awareness of need for companionship
— of need for affection — aware
of needs   (5)

7. Exclusive homosexuality — lessening identification with female
— hatred towards females di-
minishes — compares himself
more favorably with other males
— homosexuality and heterosexuality—hetehosexuality only (5.5)

8. Dreads females — focuses hatred
on mother — occasionally accepting of mother — feel equal to
women   (4.5)

9. Identifies with females — with
males   (5)

10. Relates to females as though he
were a girl friend — insight into
this — more contact with males
— relates to females as a male
                          (5)

11. Fear of male role — gradually
discloses male aspects of personality — assumes male role
                          (4.5)

requisite for work — does not
insist on suffering   (6)

Discussion of Size and Distribution of Ratings

Looking at the two sets of directions, those that attempt to convey movement of dynamics, and those that reflect the changes in work patterns, we note a positive development. The work patterns appear to have changed somewhat more incisively than the dynamics. Of the six directions established, five reflect a movement beyond five, the mid-point. It is worthwhile to note that one of the most basic work patterns, the routine writing measured by Direction IV, changed quite noticeably, the movement toward more meaningful and inspired writing being rated with seven.

There is no indication of any standstill or backward movement in the work patterns. The psychoanalytically-oriented therapy, far from interfering with the work capacity and productivity of the patient, affected work patterns favorably, for the occasional periods of standstill were always overcome. The fact that the writer now focuses on male characters, in addition to the female ones that were originally the core figures, reflects a qualitative change in the essence of writing.

As far as dynamics are concerned, we see a fair amount of change. No movement goes much beyond the mid-point of five, and five of the eleven directions are a little below mid-point. An evaluation of the figures reflects a slow progress which cannot be called steady. Almost all gains were interrupted by rather incisive backward movements. Finding the new positions uncomfortable, the patient usually slid back for a while, though never for good or even for long.

Considering how deeply ingrained the homosexuality was, it is worth noting that along all the component areas of homosexuality—dynamics directions 7, 8, 9 and 11 denote these —reasonable change was accomplished. Here then were many good beginnings, and if the project had allowed for a continuation of treatment and study of treatment beyond the allotted three years, it is very likely that a considerably greater change could have been achieved.

The directions of development in the area of dynamics are intricately woven into the changes in work patterns. For instance, details which do not show up in our tables reveal that the forward movement along work pattern direction V (the emergence of a bifocal evolvement of male and female characters in plays, stories, etc.) occurred soon after a personal experience. The writer had intercourse with a woman for the first time. Soon after he became interested in male characters in his writing, and they began to emerge for the first time. Another example was a story he wrote after working through some feelings about his mother. It concerned a terrible mother-in-law who seriously interfered in the relationship between two young people. When he completed the story, he changed the ending so that the reader would have more sympathy for the mother-in-law. It would seem at that point he forgave his own mother after the catharsis of pouring out his anger towards her.

There is also a clear-cut connection between dynamics directions 2 and 3 on the one hand, and work pattern direction III on the other. The defensive wit and hostility was reflected in the slick characters created, and when the need for clever and witty control became less pronounced and affect was freed, as indicated in dynamics direction 5, the characters and the whole nature of writing turned away from slickness.

Changes of Work Patterns

The patient produced work swiftly. His writings, in particular, were frequently accepted, produced, applauded, and adequately rewarded financially. The writer, then, did not suffer from a work block in the usual sense of having excessive difficulty creating. Yet he had various work problems, and he himself viewed and experienced them as such.

When he entered treatment he had two motivations for writing and he was conscious of both. 1) Writing was an acceptable form of rebellion. Through his writings he could express the resentment felt towards his parents, especially his mother, his rejection of human beings and his desire to keep relationships on a superficial, facetious plane in retaliation for the emotional pains endured in childhood. 2) Writing represented a means to success. The success he sought would please his ambitious mother and fulfill his own extraordinary ambition to become the great American writer. Both these motivations were, in effect, inadequate bases for continuous, high-caliber writing. The first made him evolve slick and hateful characters. The second invariably produced self-derogation.

The patient had the conscious and declared wish to reach new and better motivations through treatment. He desired to write in order to express his highly individualized ideas and what he hoped would be less rejecting interactions with people or feelings about such interaction. In substantial measure this desired motivational change did take place at the time of this evaluation. He had begun to create stories and a novel out of the urge to express his changing emotions and diversified experiences of human relationships. While he continued to write in the highly disciplined manner with which he had approached his work when he entered treatment, and while recognition and financial success remained important to him, the wish to express himself meaningfully was a powerful added motivation.

When Sam entered treatment his need for work planning was so intense as to amount to a compulsion. This compulsion churned him up and led from time to time to intense wishes of throwing off the shackles of discipline. Sometimes he actually would escape from work for weeks at a time. The intense control depressed him. When he left treatment his self-discipline, while still effective, was loosened and less tiresome. With a heightened level of emotion and impulse release there was concomitantly less depression. Looking at work pattern direction II with a rating of five, we can see that the compulsive adherence to discipline softened quite a bit, but that a certain tightness remained.

Wide swings in self-esteem as a writer existed at the beginning of treatment. While they did not stop Sam from turning out work, they did keep him from executing a cherished idea—the wish to write a novel At the end of that period of therapy which was observed through the questionnaire method, his self-esteem was heightened; he did write a novel and was very pleased with it.

The swings in self-esteem had various causes, dynamically speaking. Absorbing his mother's extraordinary ambitions for a writing career for him, Sam developed omnipotent ideas and nurtured the notion that he must write only the best. "If I don't write Hamlet I don't want to write anything, and I lacerate myself." The internalized, omnipotent desires caused much self-negation. Admiration and external acclaim—he got a good deal of applause—were often neither acknowledged nor permitted to reinforce self-esteem. There was always the gnawing thought: they do not see in me the genius I should be and therefore this success means nothing. In high school and college he was many times voted the most talented student and the person most likely to succeed, but he minimized and destroyed these honors by thinking, "This is not what I want." His ambitions, incidentally, extended not only to work but to every area of life. A first-class tennis player, he would go on the courts only if he had a perfect day and could expect to flaunt a top performance. He regarded his body as insufficiently "male" and his sexual powers as inadequate. The latter deficiency was an objective fact. These two physical shortcomings, one rather unrealistic, the other true, preyed on his mind, detracting from his self-esteem.

A further factor was that Sam was aware of the superficiality of his work. He discussed this on the basis of specific criteria. His characters were unreal, he stole from his own stories, giving later characters words and lines from earlier works, and he used writing tricks which he could enumerate and delineate. Such awareness weighed on his self-esteem. During treatment this picture changed considerably. The omnipotence diminished and his works became acceptable to him. His sexual confidence increased. His feelings became deeper and with this his writing was less contrived. The result was a more even level of self-esteem. He began to negotiate more forcefully with agents and TV executives. Where he had always expected derogation—because he though others would view his work as critically as he did —he now anticipated the generally good evaluations he obtained.

The increase in self-esteem helped him to finally start a romanic comedy, the plot of which he had long entertained in his mind. Yet there were still many fleeting, as well as clearly delineated, expectations of failure. One fantasy, for instance, focused on the opening of the story he was currently writing. In fantasy he had cast a prominent actress in the leading role. He saw her doing the part badly and imagined reviewers saying she deserved better than to be stuck in "that old clinker." A little later he fantasied getting a call from the actress, telling him not to set foot in the theater or she would walk out and never come back. After this fantasy, the writer discontinued work on the play for a short period. However, he was able to go back to it. All in all, the self-esteem was considerably enhanced, as reflected in the rating of six assigned to work pattern direction III.

During treatment two transistory changes for the worse occurred in the area of work patterns. We shall see that these relapses were the prelude to substantial improvement. The patient took more dexedrine than he had before. He also developed periods of insomnia which he connected with his work, because while he lay awake at night he worried about his writing. He could produce less well, naturally, after a relatively sleepless night. The insomnia was self-perpetuating, because an unrewarding workday after a fitful night led to more worry about work the next night and further insomnia.

The patient connected the accelerated intake of dexedrine and the insomnia with therapy, which had made him realize that much of his work was done by rote. While he was struggling, successfully as it eventually proved, to write with inspiration rather than by rote, he was in a state of anxiety about whether the transition could be made and what would be its rewards in personal satisfaction, success and money. The anxiety of the transitional phase produced insomnia and made him reach for medication. During this phase there was productivity —again work was not blocked—but there was much more re-writing than usual. The patient was unusually dissatisfied with the characters he created. "I put people into slots. I want a more human view of them. I had trouble all day with the hero; I can't make him live, I can't make him grow. Formerly I would not have wasted a thought on him. Now I can't do that. I can't let them go until they are real." The movement towards more passionate writing was one of the most accentuated, as the rating of seven in work pattern direction IV shows.

Before treatment the women in Sam's work stood out more than the men. The women acted and the men reacted to them. As the patient's conception of himself changed and he experienced himself as an active male, the roles in his plays were reversed. It should be emphasized here that creativity itself is not being described and evaluated. The effort is rather an attempt to remain within the framework of behavioral criteria, the work patterns. It should be stated that in terms of time spent on characters, as treatment progressed the writer spent more time on elaborating the male characters than before treatment. He also devoted more time to them than to the female characters. He himself generally considered this a change for the good, because he hoped that he would in time be less dissatisfied with his male characters. Yet at times he considered it a turn for the worse because he produced less material, and re-wrote almost all of it. In terms of immediate external success the change might not be seen as better. In terms of long-range work patterns it may well be considered a vast improvement.

The patient often connected writing and defecation during treatment. Such connections appeared to be genuine and to come from within rather than from analytic ideas he might have picked up in reading. He had many anal preoccupations. He evacuated his bowels many times a day and urinated often. Bathroom odors fascinated him, although they occasionally disturbed him. In general anal release rather than anal constriction was the rule, and this ties in directly with his considerable productivity. While beset by self-doubt and dissatisfaction with his work, he turned out scripts in large quantities. The over-planning, the intense discipline which he imposed on himself and which often made work a drudgery represented a form of control, acquired at a later stage than the anal one. However this was an actively anal man. He could release both his bowels and his words and ideas. The ready associations between bowel release and release of words and ideas remained unchanged. Here was a pattern that should be left intact and indeed remained so throughout treatment.

When he entered treatment, Sam was torn as to the compatibility between an emotionally palatable existence and productivity. He asked himself incessantly whether he need not suffer excruciatingly in order to be productive. Gradually he gave up the notion that he need be desperate in order to write, as work pattern direction VI suggests.

Did this patient's work patterns improve or decline? There was divided opinion in evaluating this. On the other hand, the hesitations and doubts entertained by the patient showed signs of being transitional and were giving way to the release of many new, rich and productive ideas. Also, he received higher recognition from more of his colleagues as he adopted a more serious, less glib approach.

CHAPTER 8

The Case of Brendan Daltrow, a Painter

Case Report

Like so many New Yorkers, Brendan Daltrow, a painter who came to the Arts Project at the age of twenty-six, grew up in another part of the country. The third in a family of six brothers and sisters, brought up in a tiny community on the West Coast, he had come East seeking companionship and selfrealization in the anonymity of a large city.

Of all the family, his destiny as artist and man of education had been clearly marked. He had shown talent for drawing as a child of seven and was the favorite of his mother, a hypochondriacal woman whose prime rewards in life were derived from intellectual status and the fact that she was the daughter of a school teacher. Religion was important to her. Brendan's early recollections are that she had been the more dynamic, resourceful, critical and driving parent. Mother and son shared dreams of his future accomplishments. His talent was to raise him above their life of hardship, above the laboring class of his father, a telephone maintenance man. Brendan describes him as poetic, silent and moody, detached from his children; a man with "no malice in him," who "doesn't like to tell people what to do, but who could have been a better parent." Both parents had liberal attitudes on the subject of minorities and a feeling for culture.

The patient was closest to his next younger sister, a rebel against the mother and the small town, who married the one intellectual in the town, a painter. Brendan did not think himself rebellious. "In fact, that is my trouble," he explained. "My mother instilled in me—you are not to do this or that, it isn't nice." The patient had tagged after the next older brother who would occasionally cuff him. He also had been under the authority of the oldest sister whose family role was peremptory.

Brendan had felt in his childhood that there was no one to play with, a feeling fostered by the location of his home at the end of a long lane. He was the brightest boy in class, poor at most sports except handball. Under the G.I. Bill, following a year's service in the infantry, he attended a nearby university and there became the protégé of a teacher-artist.

Although he was unfolding as a painter, these were years troubled by inner turmoil, often by a sense of disequilibrium, by loneliness and a sense of not belonging to the sophisticated and intellectual world. He experienced several episodes of panic, feelings of amorphousness and fear of being considered homosexual, though he had had no overt experiences. Despite his loneliness he made deep friendships with his colleagues, and had an intense and happy sexual relationship with a young women whom he was not ready to marry. Thus there was a disparity between his subjective sense of himself and his life in action, between his self-appraisal and the actuality.

Gaining an economic foothold in New York, which would both provide support and permit time for painting, was hard. The patient felt that apart from his art he had only menial and manual skills that thrust him back into the low occupational level of his father. But three years in New York found him prepared for a teaching career while working part-time as art-aide in the public relations department of a college.

Brendan turned to psychotherapy in May, 1955, partly, he said, because his girl friend was in therapy and seemed so assured about herself and analysis. The patient said he would like to match this—which, it soon developed, was an evasion for his own motivation and needs.

"One of my problems is getting down to paint. I paint sporadically. I feel I need to change myself to help my painting."

"Another is to make better contact with people, speaking with efficiency. And this makes it hard for me to get a job. To put it boldly—egocentricity. My girl friend thinks I am looking for perfection. And maybe I am. I feel she fails in perfection."

He was also having acute difficulties in the employment situation, was afraid of fatigue states such as he had had in college, and of having homosexual tendencies. Another motivation, he said, was, "I had always been very introverted as a child, and had always wanted to be more outgoing and analysis is sure to help."

It was felt that the strengths and potentials which would warrant psychotherapy in the Arts Project were the following. Brendan had accomplished a great deal in his life—he had become an artist of promise; he had completed his college education in the face of great poverty; he had moved toward a sustaining profession as teacher of art; he had entered a sophisticated and intellectual milieu from very different origins.

He began psychotherapy in the fall, in the aftermath of an emotional upheaval which had occurred in the summer and had left him desolated. He had the first significant love relation which terminated abruptly and left him devastated. This love affair was with a dancer who embodied every quality he longed for. Suzanne was darkly beautiful, talented, vivid, free-moving, sophisticated and from a well-to-do professional family. The relationship had ruptured, he said, because she had not been feminine and had been competitive and critical of him as a painter and man.

His painting preceding the upheaval was romantic, even lyrical, in pastels and oils of delicate color, expressed in swift and economical strokes; the themes were often figures arrested in combat as in medieval tapestry. His style and themes were individual and unswayed by the contemporary surge of abstractionism. He painted with facility, profusely though sporadically. His painting did not have the characteristics of his teacher.

At the time therapy began he was in a state of exhaustion and lassitude, with a sharp drop in creativity and productivity. He was having serious difficulty both interpersonally with his supervisor and in his work performance in the part-time job which made only slight demands on his resources as artist. He was caught in a downward spiral of wresting time and energy for painting while taking courses and working for a minimal income.

His travail manifested itself physically in his dejected bearing, a greenish pallor, wide and unalert eyes. In the waiting room, shrunken into his overcoat, hands dug into pockets, he would doze off in exhaustion.

In early therapeutic sessions it was difficult to establish a rapport and free communication with him. His voice was harsh and metallic, lacking richness and resonance. He was slow-spoken, given to long pauses, and, for many months, limited in verbal productivity. The material was presented drily, with constriction of any affect other than sarcasm, flat and colorless in detail, with a non-committal quality. He was prone to intellectualize and to talk in abstractions. He would spar verbally, countering a statement with a question. Occasionally he began a session with, "How do I know I'm getting the right therapy?" He showed an ungiving self-containment and impersonality in the therapeutic situation.

He often burdened himself by self-reproach. He called himself non-productive or not creative enough. He was frequently caught in a cycle of tardiness and absence from his job and from therapy, sometimes with a backlog of fatigue. He would then get involved with guilt for not having done his routine work well enough for his "boss."

In contrast to a preceding period where Brendan could paint with little effort, painting at that period was restricted in quantity and imagination. The figures he created were sketched in the vaguest terms and he produced incomplete cartoons with figures in rigid, arrested motion. The meaning of these sketches, according to the artist who had showed them to colleagues and galleries, did not reach nor move the onlooker. Communicative force was lacking and integrative force weaker than either in earlier and later periods. He painted at this time not so much from an inner urge as from dogged determination to carry on.

As regards the pathological patterns in Brendan's life, there were several large areas on which therapy focused. There was the dreary and totally inadequate reality of his life situation. Fundamental necessities, such as getting adequate nutrition, sleep and physical care were in total disarray, and the therapist, not agreeing with other members of the project, was convinced that these necessities should be taken care of directly without going at first to the internal causes for the low income, the poor work situation and miserable physical conditions in which the patient lived. Only after a kind of first-aid program, involving arranging for a loan for this patient, was under way were the psychodynamic causes explored.

Brendan's difficulty in communicating with the therapist, together with the sudden drop in productivity and creativity, was understood to be a sign of depression. His affect was constricted and very low.

There was no doubt that Brendan suffered from a complicated character disorder. He was an introvert and classified by his therapist as a schizoid personality. While on the one hand he had a great need for aloneness during which he could be creatively engaged, he also had an urgent need for company, which he had difficulty securing because of his withdrawn nature, his sarcastic approach to others and his many other interpersonal difficulties.

Sad, and occasionally touching, was the patient's constant struggle with time. He treated time like an enemy. He was continually late for work, for appointments with friends, for meetings with art dealers and for his therapeutic appointments. When late he was always on the defensive. He performed his job unsatisfactorily and was often reprimanded by his employer. All the patterns interacted. Because of his lateness and poor work performance he felt guilty towards the supervisor and coped with the latter's criticisms in both a defensive and offensive manner. The widespread uneasiness all these difficulties created made it more difficult for him to concentrate on painting. In this respect Brendan seemed distinctly different from several other artists in the Project who were discussed by the therapists, supervisors and research people. For some of the others found refuge from the strains of their life in painting. They painted in order to be relieved of the tensions of everyday life. Brendan, on the other hand, did not look upon painting as a refuge. It was available to him only if the rest of his life was in relatively good shape.

Brendan usually related to authority figures in an argumentative way rather than with realistic appraisal and assertiveness. But these traits were sometimes expressed with more courage and rebelliousness than he gave himself credit for. In one laboring job he had protested because a Negro workman was not getting a raise when he, Brendan, had been given one and because of the objections he was discharged. Honest and self-reliant as the patient could be in the case of social injusties, he noted that he took on others' opinions in cultural matters, without any direct appraisal of his own feelings. Another aspect of this uncertainty and lack of identity was his wish to have the analyst tell him things, because, "I have thought that in associating with a very superior person some of that superiority will come me."

Superiority feelings and sarcasm and refusal of simple courtesies were frequent and represented a cover for his low self-esteem and his difficulty in maintaining a footing with his associates. He would get into difficulty with men at social gatherings by flirting with their girl friends or wives. He could declare his unpopular ideas but would be nonplussed at the reactive hostility directed toward him. His sarcasm often was witty and he could write scathing, clever satire.

He was precise and observant of slights others committed, but unaware of his own. He was afraid of being "taken," but kept his records and bills in such disorder that he could not check their accuracy. He came late for sessions but was watchful lest the analyst cut his time.

Brendan had deep concern and deep confusion and conflict about aggressiveness, violence, force and forcefulness, passivity and assertiveness.

"I have the desire to be a powerful person—I don't think I can ever be a nasty person who is not liked; but I can never become a positive force and manage people."

He had long been fascinated and "bothered" by violence as expressed in *Streetcar Named Desire* and in *Duel in the Sun*. He gradually realized that rather than brute force, what he admired in these movies was the characters' "knowing where they're going—I don't feel comfortable with them because I lack direction. I sense a confusion between violence and holding to direction."

Retaliatory violence towards his girl friend, Suzanne, was expressed in some dreams: "In Morocco at a riverbank I toss Suzanne into the river because she is being nasty to me about returning and about my painting. Then some characters pull me up on the riverbank and struggle with me, with knives and sickles; we are interlocked."

This brought to his mind a folksong, which he chanted:
I sat by my love—
My love fell asleep.
I stabbed her with a dagger
And I threw her in the river.
It was a dreadful sight.

Another such dream was that he picked up a rock and said to Suzanne, who was lying in the road and had said she wasn't sure he loved her, "I'll smash your head if you don't believe me."

He distrusted his gentleness and capacity for tenderness. He suspected that they represented weakness and an incapacity for masculine force and violence. Yet violence and force revolted him. The fear of being aggressive as forerunner to violence contributed to his passivity, unassertiveness and muted hostility.

It is interesting that this preoccupation expressed itself in his paintings in two ways: in the choice of themes and in the movement of figures. He started and left unfinished many paintings of war. They usually turned into arrangements of figures arrested in motion. All of his human figures at this time were constrained, their arms, as it were, bound to their sides, a self-paralysis designed to stave off violence. Brendan's art instructors had also been concerned with the problem of brutality and control through rigidity, which his art form expressed.

Brendan Daltrow was obsessed with a fear of homosexuality which at times seemed to blend into the confusions about aggression. It was a harassing preoccupation, occasionally deepening into panic because he anticipated being thought homosexual. Actually outside of one passive experience as an adolescent with an aggressive older cousin he had experienced only fantasies and fears. He dated the onset of the preoccupation to the time, in college, when rumors were spread about his being homosexual. Soon afterward he was upset at feeling that it would be exciting to hold a young sailor's penis and get him excited. He said: "I got into a crazy dreamlike state. I went to bed feeling half out of my mind and the whole thing passed. . . . But when I came to New York and went out on the street in my lunch hour there were a lot of pretty girls around. I seemed to be someone in a sea of breasts and bellies and bare arms. So there I was interested in women and I was reassured. Several men tried to pick me up but I was terrified and never gave an inch to any of them."

Generally the fantasies were of his being receptive and submissive, which he termed being the woman. In one dream he turned into a woman: "I was back home and there was a tree —an apple tree. My father, and I think my older brother, were there, and this tree was not symmetrical, it needed trimming. And my father said it had to be cut off, and I didn't agree with him, in a half-rebellious way."

"Then I was up in the tree trimming it; and then I am a girl and myself—I am conscious of being a girl and talking. I am the girl and nude and conscious of being looked at, and I have the feeling of pleasure in my body. I am trying to cut off the limb which comes around in such a way that I am unable to saw it off. Afterwards I feel sort of knocked out."

He had the dream in which he submitted with muted rebellion. In the dream he lacked self-assertiveness, and when he woke up he had some confusion about sexual identity. He felt that any lack of assertiveness to girls was a masculine weakness and revealed an effeminate condition. He said: "Related to this is something like this equation; aggressiveness and strength equal masculinity, passivity and weakness equal femininity. And playing the masculine role is taking the initiative just in meeting girls."

The homosexuality constellation became accentuated during great fatigue, or when he was depleted after days of inadequate eating. He then would speak in a thin childish whine. However, as soon as he had slept and had some meals, he would be preoccupied with the attractive girls he glimpsed and would present as a problem in his sessions how to make their acquaintance and sleep with them. His manner at these times would be more forthright and dynamic, and his speech more forceful and fuller bodied. The fantasies based on fleeting views of the girls would be expressed in quick, easily-produced sketches.

Also there were fantasies of being in a sexual relationship with a woman in which he was babied, coddled and cuddled, a relationship in which he was the receiver and in that sense dependent. In contrast to the distaste and fear of exploitation in the homosexual fantasies, these were gratifying and not disturbing. The significance of these fantasies appeared to the therapist to be the following: one important component was Brendan's fear of male aggression directed toward him and culminating in the anal invasion of sexual intimacy. To relieve anxiety he craved nurturing from a woman which was expressed in the vision of a great mythic mother who gives all, including sexual union. In the actual experience of sexual intercourse Brendan was, before therapy and early in therapy, subject to premature ejaculation. He had described Suzanne as being unfeminine and aggressive and said that therefore he had moved toward the parting. It later appeared that his sexual difficulty had played a disturbing role in their relationship and had reinforced his doubt about his masculinity and his anxiety about being homosexual and not sufficiently masculine to satisfy his passionate partner.

We shall now turn to the changes that occurred during treatment. First there is the depressive constellation which was strongly accentuated when the patient broke with Suzanne. This had accentuated the repressive self-control since the painter intensified control over his aggression, thereby muting almost all other affect as well. His depressive tendencies were always intensified when a threat to his status existed, for the painter attributed all difficulty with people to a lack of proper family status. This emphasis grew out of his mother's derogatory attitude toward the father's status as a member of the working class. Early in therapy the depressive tendencies manifested themselves in a loss of direction and drive, in quiet despair and self-recriminations. The depression affected Brendan as an artist for it lead to a paucity of imagery and constriction of forms.

We can trace the lack of effectiveness and the concomitant lack of self-assertiveness in various comments made by the patient. He said: "I do hold my energy back. I can walk down the street and feel very much that I love everyone, but no one would even suspect it from my deadpan. . . . If I stay behind a stone wall and don't do anything no one can attack me."

"When other people get angry, I freeze. I remember when I was a child I was not so deadpan, I was not so stingy about doing something for people. . . . In the second grade I became an outsider. . . . I remember my mother telling me, keep quiet, that I was making myself the center of attention. She said, 'People like you if you do that (remain quiet).' "

"I think the one time I was not holding my energies back was what I call my halcyon period. I was killing myself with painting. . . . That was when I first came to New York."

As the comments suggest, Brendan, when he entered therapy, was aloof and appeared detached, urgent though his wish was to establish friendships and be close to others. What impressed the observer was a total lack of warmth. But both the depressive feelings and the constriction of affect improved. It took approximately twelve months for the first noticeable changes to occur, but once they were under way improvement, with sporadic exceptions, was continual. The depressive feelings lifted. Brendan had more drive to take care of household and physical needs. His appetite improved. There was a return of "zest" for sex. At no time was there the "irreality," the episodes of dissociation, which had occurred in college days and immediately after.

Affective freedom was increasing. In the sessions he laughed spontaneously and showed a sense of humor, and was more open in expressing embarrassment or shame about events in which, in retrospect, he hadn't liked his own behavior. He showed more tenderness and less sentimentality in talking about the family failures. However, there never was a strong emotional expression such as weeping or open anger. His defensiveness had greatly decreased and his talking was less impersonal.

Eventually depressive feelings diminished in intensity and frequency to such an extent that during a five-month period in which questionnaire data were collected he had only two brief runs of depression. His cycles of tardiness and oversleeping after staying up much of the night were shorter. Then once more the depressive feelings that had diminished flared up with anxiety, which Brendan was quite open in voicing, when a case of iritis called for cessation of all work and all use of the eyes and increased his financial difficulties. His tardiness, however, had changed remarkably to promptness.

Essentially there was little sense of fatigue. For a time he hadn't slept well with the rigors of adjusting to a new job. These strains certainly contributed to the onset of the iritis.

After the iritis he still had brief bouts of mild depression accompanied by self-reproach for not painting, making little allowance for his work schedule. Sometimes depression shifted into a sense of agitation, or of "spinning." In general, though, the depressive constellation had given way to an overall mild optimism.

As to Brendan's detachment and apparent coldness, it was the therapist's sense that the patient had suffered from an actual deficit of emotional nurture from his family, that he attempted to meet their vociferous dependency needs, and that he compensated for his deprivation and their demands by his own wish to be babied, expressed in fantasies and in his sexual intimacy with women. However, when he was confronted by the emotional needs of these women he pulled away, often by putting up a cold wall of alienating "honesty." Another contrast was shown with some waiflike young women with whom he did not have a sexual relationship and to whom he was protective and helpful in their emotional difficulties.

Towards the middle of the second year of treatment affective freedom was increasing, chiefly in the direction of competent self-assertiveness in the face of aggression.

Brendan's manner to the analyst was warmer but the verbal content interpersonally was unchanged. He did make an occasional friendly general remark and indicated respect for her opinion to the extent of asking her for her reaction to, say an exhibit, or an article about art. Next the affective range became much improved and quite a number emerged. There was on the whole a diminution of tension.

In the second year of therapy Brendan made large strides with regard to the authority relationship to his job and supervisor. In this year he accepted his responsibility to the job and worked out a schedule in which he was more dependable. He mended the previously friction-laden personal relationship with the supervisor. The relation to authority figures in the family changed as well in this phase of therapy. He no longer sulked in covert rebellion against his seniors but met difficulties with open discussion.

The parents ceased to be authorities to him, but he was careful not to admit to them that he saw their faults and shortcomings. He began to see his mother as a tired, whining hypochondriac, implied by illustrative incidents rather than by definite statement. The older sister, who had once brought down this mother's wrath on six-year-old Brendan for his sexual activity, remained an important authority in the family and would write to him complaining of family mishaps, asking him to intervene to change the behavior of the other children toward the mother. The patient began to recognize her attempt to control at long distance and wrote to her that their mother had had a part in evoking these difficulties.

In this year also, he developed insight into the intellectual authority he ascribed to and resented in his painter brother-in-law, Don. During a six-week period when Brendan was host to his brother-in-law, he saw him with increasing clarity and handled himself very well with Don. He also was protective and helpful, taking Don's paintings to various galleries to help him get a show.

At first Brendan had been snobbish about his supervisor on artistic grounds, but the man's helpfulness was so generous that the patient developed genuine liking for him and accepted invitations to his home.

His previously repressed aggression to other men, especially his peers, came through not only in his sarcasm but in his holding to his position in arguing as well. He quoted them as saying that he was assertive and critical, though he commented he did not see himself that way. He took assertiveness to be a verbal "telling people off" when they "impose" on him. He took the freedom to be brusque as self-assertiveness. Once his breaking through physical restraint took the form of teasing at a New Year's Eve party, and he bumped into people as he danced, different from his usual "polite" self. When homosexual passes were made to him to which he felt no response, he was puzzled as to whether he should rebuff the man verbally or "punch him in the nose."

He increasingly asserted himself directly against minor aggressions of everyday life (as against taxi-drivers!) He began outbursts at tradespeople who treated him unjustly or who imposed on him. He became aware that these episodes occurred especially when he felt frustrated. Brendan recognized that some of his confusion and conflict about aggressiveness and brutality stemmed from his mother's teaching that "nice people don't . . ." with which she had interrupted his spontaneous fights with other boys. She had left him no defense against an older brother whose butt he had often been.

In treatment his assertiveness in communication was developing. He no longer would ask for direction for what to talk about. He began to declare himself in a clear manner when his views differed, instead of assuming a strained silence. He initiated the move to use the couch. His manner became easier and more friendly.

During this time he was preoccupied with fantasies of shooting indiscriminately, which changed to a specific impulse to shoot at electric bulbs. He told of having a dream in which for the first time he shot a gun with successful aggressiveness. His dreams usually were long and intricate, charged with meaning but worked through reluctantly.

Brendan also began to attribute some of his preoccupation with aggressiveness to the semi-skilled laborers with whom he had worked for years and with whom he felt unsure. A later element appeared bound to a philosophy about aggression, a "Nietzcheanism" and cynicism, derived from Don, whom he had greatly admired and whose sarcastic views on life and women he had adopted, as he was prone to do with "superior" people.

As treatment progressed Brendan developed a real sense of himself and of mastery of work and painting. He was little preoccupied with righting the wrongs that people did to him, and no longer found it necessary to have defensive arguments with tradespeople. He was sarcastic on only a few occasions, once toward a girl who ridiculed his painting. The fantasy of shooting vanished.

As to sexual problems the fear of homosexuality continued to be fused with the aggression constellation. Brendan's dreams and fantasies often contained references to homosexuality and to aggression in the way that a phallic symbol, as a knife or club, in his possession, suddenly became limp. They did not show a masochistic deep-seated acceptance of another's aggression toward himself; he wished but did not know how to ward aggressiveness off.

It is interesting that his sarcasm which was accentuated when he dealt with women, was revealed in an insight to be a cover-up for ejaculation praecox, another problem in the sexual area. He discovered that he had at least the power to *reject* if not to *fulfill*. In the second year of treatment he attained a stable close relationship with a young woman, a painter, with sexual fulfillment for both.

He stated that he envisaged himself occasionally in the girl's sexual role. This could not be taken in a literal sense until he gave more information about his homosexual fantasies. It remained noteworthy that these fantasies became more active during periods of great fatigue and shortage of funds.

There was no indication that Brendan identified with the "powerful mother." Identification with the "weak father" was expressed only in terms of fear that he would be a dull, nonproductive, inarticulate person like his father. There was no indication at this point that this was on a specific sexual basis, rather it was in terms of general activity.

For a long time in treatment there was essentially no movement in Brendan's preoccupation with homosexuality. He presented a minimum of material. It was far less available for discussion than such matters as his work habits and relationships at work.

How complicated this problem was and how it merged with the areas of aggression and authority is indicated in the final part of a terror dream representing his supervisor as a military authority and himself appearing for inspection unprepared, unshaven, sloppily dressed.

"And this is the meaningful part. . . . I began to look at my legs and I think they are feminine, they are so soft. . . . I go racing away. I am terrified. . . . I race through a cornfield. . . . It's a very lovely beautiful morning and I have a mood of enjoying it, of having a feeling to go with this. I leap up in the air and have the feeling like treading water in the air, which I often have in dreams. I start following one of the branches of the tree to the trunk. I begin to feel that this is a dream but at the same time I am doing this. It's a very tall tree, almost as an act of vision I get the view of this tree. . . . The leaves are a sort of green, and beautiful. I start sliding down this trunk and I start getting sexually excited and I awake and have an orgasm."

When Brendan was with his employer he saw himself as feminine and was afraid that the man would consider him homosexual.

By the end of the second year of treatment, Brendan's sexual functioning was improved. There no longer were premature ejaculations. His relationship was centered on the same girl, Dorothy. It was still a steady relationship, though "low-keyed" and sometimes on the verge of separation.

At the end of treatment Brendan's reality situation, that is the situation in which he lived, had improved tremendously. And so had his psychodynamic patterns. Real and favorable changes were manifest in every area. He had developed greater ease and poise, genuine self-assurance about taking onto himself appropriate authority in his classes with his colleagues among the teachers. He no longer was shrill and constrained. He rationalized less and displayed a genuine sense of humor. He showed warmth toward his students and had increased in maturity. He displayed initiative and originality in coping with student problems. He felt fatherly to some of the youths, particularly those who had been failing in their studies.

He spoke much more briskly and quick-wittedly. He had a sense of being in command of himself and spoke in a fuller voice and more spontaneously. He was prompt and "on the ball." His clothes had become more conventional; a hat instead of a beret was a conscious break from the convention of the artist. "The hell with it, what people think about my wearing a hat— I need a hat to keep my ears warm." He was more at ease with the school people although he was occasionally embarrassed when he told artists about teaching—again a status problem. He gave his first party at Christmas and enjoyed playing host.

There no longer appeared to be any difficulty with relationship to authority figures in the teaching situation. In fact there was little difficulty in the aggression-passivity constellation. His protectiveness of "nebisches" turned towards a more clear-cut way of relating to people, which was striking in relation to his agitated, irritating, talented brother-in-law. He became gentle and supportive without mockery or attack. On the other hand, he continued to be touchy about pretentiousness and posing in girls. Nevertheless, on the whole women liked him, "once you get to know him, he has a wonderful personality." There was no one he moved toward who had the quality Suzanne had possessed.

There were no significant new relationships with either men or women, though he had occasional fleeting social and sexual relationships with girls and had several artist friends. He linked his wanting "someone who is warm and not cool" with his feeling of getting less detached.

He seemed to have achieved individuation from his father and no longer emphasized status as the chief explanation for events in his life. His self-appraisal in interpersonal matters had become much more accurate. A great deal of warmth that he received during the iritis and the modest money-gift that he was given by the teachers in his department completely dispelled his cynicism about the goodness of people. In his buoyancy he brought the analyst two lush persimmons, telling her that the world had become a friendly place.

Brendan became less concerned with painting as a means of rebellion or of conformity than as a way of finding his own reality. He did not like the so-called "New York group" because, he said, "they have not painted out of love, but out of trying to be different." He granted them courage in doing that, but this was not his goal for himself. He wanted to paint whatever his image was, without pushing it into the issue of conformity or rebellion.

He consistently maintained that he was a very good painter and accepted as part of how he worked the fact that there were low periods and active, exhilarated periods. The one area of security he had was as artist. There, he stated, he felt that he was himself.

The inability to complete a painting when he was artistically excited was often not a matter of work block but of interruption of the mood by getting ready to go to work. When he yielded to the mood, he completed the drawing and the painting, but at the cost of being up all night and then oversleeping. There were periods of artistic inaction—with depression, fatigue, pre-occupation with other duties. Rather than painting sporadically, which he had complained of when he applied for therapy, he assumed a pattern of long periods of inaction and long periods of painting. No connection with premature ejaculation was established.

Painting in part compensated for lack of full gratification from women and expressed his conflict about violence rather than anxiety, but it also had a life of its own. He painted in an inspirational frame of mind and more freely when unharried by his feeling of obligation and depression. His inspiration might be a vista or a glimpse of a desirable woman. He was rather sad at being out of step with expressionism but felt that his only course was to paint as he felt at a particular time. The painting reflected contact with real life and was not a with-drawal from experience. One theme that long engaged him was trees in their various moods, painted without sentimentality.

Half-starved, self-negligent, impoverished at the beginning of treatment, he identified with his passive, weary father, he had expected rejection as painter, person and lover. With the ac-complishment of his plan to become an art teacher he found that he enjoyed the interaction with the children. He liked them, he liked his colleagues, and he enjoyed the sense of hav-ing economic and social stability beyond his father's. His tensions and despairs diminished. And above all he painted pro-lifically and with sponteneity.

Predictions

Prediction #1

The patient overestimates the role of his humble social origins and does not face the importance which interpersonal inter-actions within the family play in personality development. This makes for a fatalistic, static picture. *As he comes to a new realization he will be freer in all conceptualizing and in ex-periencing his emotions without distortion and displacement. This expansion should enliven his creative expression.*
Results: *This prediction came true.*

Prediction #2

As Brendan resolves his problems with people in authority, *his paid work for self-support will be at lesser cost of emotional energy and thereby a lesser drain on his creative energy.*
Results: *This prediction came true.*

Prediction #3

As he works out the components of his depression, especially as aggression becomes overt, *he will have greater freedom of imagination and greater energy at his disposal. His painting will have more freedom and inner movement.*
Results: *This prediction came true.*

Prediction #4

As he develops his own self-assertiveness and confidence in his reactions *he will crave less prodding from outside.* The relation-ship with Suzanne has been an expression of his admiration for aggressiveness and power. As his own assertiveness develops *he will be less dependent emotionally for these qualities in another person.*
Results: *This prediction came true.*

Directions of Development and Ratings

Dynamics

1. Long and frequent depressions — occasional depressions — mild depressions and self-reproach — occasional periods of agitation (5)

2. Shifting of affects (love and aggression) — some affect emerging in transference — broader range of affect (5)

3. Argumentative with authority figures — reappraisal of boss — of parents and siblings — realistic appraisal of authority figures (8)

4. Repressed aggression — open aggression with associated feelings of violence — assertion (9)

5. Contacts with others through defensive sarcasm — insight into identification with s a r c a s t i c brother-in-law — flare-up of sarcasm towards women — lessening of sarcasm (7)

6. Fear of homosexuality — increased assertiveness toward men and women — heterosexuality established (5)

7. Ejaculatia praecox — adequate functioning (8)

8. Superiority feelings t o w a r d s teachers and colleagues — awareness of underlying inferiority — sense of equality (5)

9. Indecision, obsessional doubts — purposeful behavior (6)

Work Patterns

I. Difficulty in accessibility of imagery, form — can reach and find form and color (8)

II. Fatigue — aggressive drives freed, less fatigue — no fatigue (8)

III. Perfectionism in work — exultation in work (8)

IV. Rebellion primary motivation of work — works autonomously (8)

V. Self-image of "genius" alter- n a t i n g with self-image of "nothing" — stability of self-image (6)

VI. Reluctant to show paintings — shows paintings easily (7)

Discussion of Size and Distribution of Ratings

This patient developed quite markedly within the area of work and work patterns. With regard to personality development we see a uniform though not as conspicuous picture of forward movement. Again, as in all the other areas discussed, restriction of affect is among those problems least given to improvement through psychotherapy, as is evident by a rating of five along Direction of Development in Dynamics #2. It is interesting, however, that in the terms of physical change, where improvements are difficult to obtain, the patient did very well. For we see from Direction of Development in Dynamics #7 that the difficulties which he had with ejaculatia praecox ceased almost completely.

At the end of treatment Brendan Daltrow was a man with few work difficulties. This does not necessarily mean that he was a great painter, for we are measuring by our directions of development merely attitudes towards work, that is, aspects of the creative process but not the creative products, which critics have enough difficulty in evaluating for a given era, regardless of how extremely ambiguous the evaluation is in a long-term view. But this patient's working difficulties, which were tremendous when he entered treatment, disappeared almost completely. We see that the lowest rating attaches to Direction of Development in Work Patterns V (self-image alternates between seeing himself as genius or nothing). The rating of six attributed to that dimension is not very low, a fact which indicates that the painter was more stable as far as his self-esteem was concerned. Knowing how creative people, even the most stable, waver in the evaluation of their work, it is considered great improvement that this man's self-evaluation became as stabilized as the rating reflects.

Both the problem of fatigue in work, which was bound up with Directions of Development in Dynamics 2 and 4 and which was the primary difficulty which Brendan Dartlow faced as an artist, disappeared almost completely. He entered psychoanalytic psychotherapy a man who worked most sporadically. He left almost free from fatigue and could work more or less at will.

Changes of Work Patterns

Outstanding in this case were alternations between freezing and explosions of feeling and imagery. The explosions always yielded a profusion of creative productions. The paralyzation of feeling was expressed as follows: "I am fatigued. I feel empty. I feel a deep passivity. I cannot paint." The other extreme, which took the form of volcanic release, was also described in detail: "I got excited by painting last night. A vision broke through. I painted for hours. I didn't want to stop. I felt like I do in some of my dreams. In these dreams I want to shoot, I have the impuse to smash, to strike out. That's what it feels like when my visions break through. When I say to my girl, 'I hate you,' that is when things break through. When I get a red, charged image out on paper I feel like crying."

The alternation between the experience of breaking forth, exploding, wishing to smash and strike out, and feelings of emptiness and paralysis, derived in this case from the alternation between impulse release and impulse control. Because of intense desires to smash and strike out, Brendan had to put tight controls on his emotions. But in this, as in many other cases, the controls were not selective. Not only the aggressive impulses were kept in check but all emotion, imagery and creative urges as well.

The described pattern did indeed represent an unconsciously self-imposed block. Thus, in this instance the label "work block" is accurate.

We note that during treatment a change for the better occurred with regard to the heavy restraints which Brendan imposed on his aggressive impulses, on other feelings, and on his imagery. The severe block was ameliorated as the ratings show. When Brendan's feelings, images and energy were checked by the unconsciously-imposed inner controls, he was subjectively fatigued. He felt undernourished and deprived of energy. The patient connected his fatigue with practical, external deprivations and not with internal processes. However, the fatigue was caused by the battle that went on between the forces that put the brakes on his aggression and all his other feelings and the forces that pressed for release in the form of creative work, living experiences and self-expression. The patient's explanations for the causes of his fatigue were rationalizations that concealed the unconscious processes. The painter, however, resisted insight and clung to his rationalizations throughout treatment. Though he improved, he did not ever admit the true motivation of the subjectively and painfully experienced sense of tiredness.

The patient often wavered between the assumption that he was a genius and the conviction that he was nothing. In either of these extreme states he was unproductive. When he believed himself to be a genius none of his own creative productions met with his approval. There was self-censure and physical destruction of his work or other forms of erasure of what he created. When he felt like nothing he was too depressed to approach the studio and the paints and express himself.

Among the motivations for Brendan Daltrow's creative expression economic and libidinal deprivation played a considerable role. The specific form this took was that he created in his paintings from time to time the objects he lacked in real life. For instance sometimes if he could not have a beautiful woman he would paint one instead. This form of finding gratification alternated with depression as a reaction to deprivation.

The patient discussed four prime motivations for his being engaged creatively. 1) To paint the content of wish-fulfilling fantasies, that is, to paint from time to time those situations or objects which he could not obtain in reality. This motivation was at work less frequently than motivations 2, 3 and 4, and according to the artist did not lead to works of as good caliber as motivations 2, 3 and 4 did. This motivation was somewhat diminished during treatment and the other three motivations increased in importance. The researchers were not convinced that the change from painting as direct need gratification to painting as separate from direct need gratification necessarily constituted a forward movement. 2) Brendan painted when he found himself preoccupied with inner images, experiencing a need to get them out and articulate them. This sustained his creative periods most, was the source of what he believed were his best works, and also led to painting without an accompanying sense of guilt. 3) There was an enjoyment of playing with form and design on canvas. This motivation led to work of a more technical kind which Brendan considered to be less lastingly satisfactory than pictures created with motivation 2. 4) The painter used his art to accentuate his movement away from his California small-town background. His father was to him a symbol of stagnation and failure. He felt compelled to grow beyond this, and used painting to assure his own status as a man of intelligence, imagination and free spirit. His father, interestingly enough, encouraged his son's use of art as a means of separating himself from the family's dull, middle-class background. This last motivational force was accepted by the patient without guilt. It proved productive and was never questioned either by him or his therapist.

The patient wavered frequently—at least once a month—between the intention to give up painting and the conviction that painting was his prime satisfaction in life. Thus he often returned to his painting as though he were a newcomer to it.

CHAPTER 9

Summary

Increased Mental Health Improves Artistic Work Habits

The assembled data and measurements show that the productivity of the artists whom we observed was not affected negatively by psychoanalytic therapy. The age-old fear that the artist who gets emotionally well ceases to create proved groundless. Quite to the contrary, both with regard to quantity of output and with regard to the constructiveness and appropriateness of the work patterns which we studied in detail there was positive development. In many areas notable and decisive improvements occurred and were recorded. As a matter of fact the improvements obtained were even more marked than our study shows. Our research funds allowed us to study the artist patients during a period of roughly three years. Data and measurements presented were extrapolated from treatments during such three-year periods. Actually, nearly all artists remained in treatment beyond the observation period covered in this report, financing therapy themselves. In all cases substantial further gains were made during these subsequent, privately-financed therapy periods, and Case 5, who had only come along slowly, made great strides from the third year on. Specifically the following steps were taken: Matthew Taylor has become a most productive sculptor, with decisively reduced work difficulties; Jonathan Norton similarly has continued to produce more than before therapy and with greater fluidity; Tina Mandell's productivity and work patterns have remained relatively even but she has exhibited more than during therapy because she is more active and more practical about placing her work in exhibitions; Samuel Ellington is a productive, well-established writer with excellent work habits. Moreover he has become a married man.

[163]

Lewis Nordlund has had a rather notable success in motion pictures with much favorable criticism. Brendan Daltrow is much improved as a person and creative man.

In the majority of cases the ratings describing the forward movement in work patterns are higher than those describing the forward movement as far as development of the total personality is concerned. Of course we must remember that the answers that described movement in work patterns were supplied by the patients, while the answers that described forward movement in personality development were supplied by the therapists. Yet, as stated, the questions called for answers so specific and so behavioral that it is unlikely to assume that a higher degree of optimism shown by the patients, as compared with the therapists, accounts for the differences in the two fields in which ratings were collected. Rather our conclusions are that the persons treated and observed changed more deeply in their attitudes towards work than in the many other areas of personality.

Another way of putting it is that any changes in psychic balance, in the defense structure, in identification, self-esteem, etc. were first reflected in the work patterns. If one of our artists, for example, was able to make a correction in his identification—say feel more male, more prepared to fill the sexual role demanded of him by constitution and society—a healthy change in identification and subsequent increases in self-esteem affected the approach to the work first and social patterns later. The work patterns were most accessible to emotional-mental shifts. Creative work has some of the aspects of play, even though it demands a higher degree of discipline than play. We note in the play of children that they will imbue their play with new stirrings, new anticipations, new perceptions and new attitudes before such novel mental-emotional products are released in other areas of self-realization and self-expression. The play of children, at one and the same time highly private and highly expressive, is the forerunner, so it seems, of creative activity. The latter, too, reflects new attitudes before these attitudes permeate other areas of functioning.

Among the various dramatic illustrations of the above point

let us focus on the manifestation of excessive control through rigidity and compulsiveness. Several artist patients complained of a state of being bogged down in ritual to the point where spontaneity was scarce, primarily because in inhibiting aggressive and sexual impulses that were sensed to be dangerous the individual inhibited the entire emotional life. All of our artists suffered in varying though always rather conspicuous degrees from lack of spontaneity and the concurring rigidity. Matthew Taylor, Case 1, reported the existence of a hairline balance between drive and control, a constant battle between explosive ideas and the immediate compulsive need for extinction of the idea. This see-saw alternation between drive and defense was represented graphically in an oppressive preoccupation with symmetry. It illuminates our point that the compulsive insistence on symmetry disappeared in his work to a degree where we gave this development a rating of 8—that is a near-total change was observed The parallel development in human relations where it was a question of releasing more emotion and using less constricting intellectualizing that served as defense achieved only a rating of 6.5.

The second artist, Jonathan Norton, went through a similar development. When he entered treatment his control over affect was revealed workwise as a ponderous approach to the canvases. In human relationships it appeared as intellectualization. At the end of our observation period the ponderous approach had given way to fluidity to a degree where the optimal rating of 9 was applied. However, intellectualizing in relations to wife, child, friends and students was reduced somewhat less conspicuously. The development there rated a 7.5 figure. In Tina Mandell rigidity was originally equally pronounced both in her social relations and in her work, and gave way to fluidity in equal measure in both areas. Samuel Ellington, the writer in our project, was able at the end of the observation period to be considerably more flexible in his work schedule without neglecting his work. A previous sense of compulsion was gone and hence an inner rebelliousness about having to work disappeared. In the areas of personal relations there was also a reduction of rigidity but it was not as conspicuous as that noted in the approach to work. Finally, Brendan Daltrow, Case 6, shows a more fluctuating pattern. Some affects, e.g., aggression, were totally freed in social behavior by the end of the observation period, while a mild affective constriction, which in his case lead to the symptom of fatigue, was still noticable in his approach to his work.

Sublimation of Aggression

As we see, in all cases a variety of work problems and personality difficulties sprang from powerfully stored quantities of aggression which were inhibited, sometimes projected upon others, and at times covered up by reaction formations in the form of politeness, helpfulness, general pleasantness. Only when the controls were lifted and the artists became both more aware of their aggression and also more able to express aggression and opposition, did work difficulties in the form of lethargy, tightness, or depression disappear. Like other patients who seek psychotherapeutic help, the artist patients were prompted in their desire to change emotionally by many symptoms that were the outcome of repressed aggression. They experienced latent irritation towards and resentment of family members and colleagues, depressions, and sense of failure as human beings and productive individuals. However, what distinguished them from the non-artist patient was the fact that they invariably sought out their productive work as a chief means whereby to cope with frustration and aggression. Art was an acceptable expression of revolt as in the case of the writer Samuel Ellington; or it was a means of competing with a powerful rival as in the case of Jonathan Norton. Tina Mandell resorted to art as a means of dissociating herself from her conventional parents whom she resented deeply and who ridiculed, misunderstood and underestimated her work. For Brendan Daltrow, too, rebellion was the primary motivation for work when he first entered treatment. Only gradually did other motivations become more prominent and meaningful. What separated our artist patients from other patients was the fact that rebellion lead them not to sheer hatred and pure withdrawal from the world but rather to the idea that in withdrawing from a world they did not like they could create one that they could both control and cherish. Where other patients frequently withdraw into apathy and nurse destructive thoughts, the anger of these artist patients lead to construction and creation. In all cases the creations became bolder, bigger and more clearly delineated when the affect of anger was freed and the artist could draw on it freely. Matthew Taylor, Jonathan Norton, Tina Mandell and Brendan Daltrow made larger and bolder pictures as their treatment progressed. Samuel Ellington, the writer, literally wrote a bigger piece, namely a novel, as the results of therapy mounted.

The process here described represents a very special form of sublimation. Sublimation consists of changes in aim or object or both aim and object without a blocking of drive energy (4). What characterizes the sublimations which the artists here studied performed was: 1) the fact that aggression invariably played a focal role in the orientation towards creativity. All of our artist patients resorted to productivity and creativity as a means of sublimating aggressive energies in the sense of changing the aim. Instead of destroying objects they made objects, lured them out of canvas, clay, or out of paper and typewriter. When energies were released rather than inhibited the work patterns were affected most favorably. In other words, the freeing of aggressive energies greatly advanced the capacity to work. 2) The objects upon whom aggression was originally focused were changed in keeping with the demand of sublimation, but the changes were very specific ones. Invariably the object was expanded enormously. Instead of one or a few substitute objects the artist patients introduced a new universe of objects and moreover saw to it that these universes were in a state of change. In the case of the very gifted Matthew Taylor, for instance, the original objects, namely father and mother, towards whom aggression had been directed, were replaced in the artist's world by animal objects. Matthew Taylor, before therapy and in the earlier phases of therapy, created primarily animal sculptures. Later he made representations and variations of human figures. Analytic psychotherapy had helped him to widen the range of objects significantly.

Omnipotent Fantasy, a Prominent Work Hurdle

The artist patients with the exception of only one, namely Tina Mandell, had grandiose ideas concerning their talents and their products. Having produced notable works that had found acclaim, they had their eyes fixed on ever more outstanding artistic successes. Invariably such ambitions lead to an intensification of narcissistic expectations. The focus on objects and on the creation of a universe of objects was obscured. In the case of Lewis Nordlund, the actor-singer, acting and singing were activities which at first were undertaken to a large degree to serve the patient's narcissistic needs for praise. Self-directedness in the form of experienced inner promptings and emotions was rather low. The patient experienced the concern with praise from an audience in the form of intense self-consciousness which interfered with his performances. For when he performed he was divided between self-expression and a vigilance as to how such self-expression was accepted. His attention shifted from performance to an inquiry as to how the performance was accepted minute by minute. The actor-singer's self-consciousness improved in some measure when this split in attention was reduced by his growing ability to fuse the two focal points, namely his own performance and the recipient audience. This occurred when his concern with the audience while still existent took on a more marginal character in the sense of a dimmer, more generalized, preoccupation with the listeners and a clearer concentration on the vocal, mental, producing self.

Nearly all the artists destroyed too many works before and in the early phases of treatment because they were intent on producing masterpieces and felt—often in retrospect wrongly —that created pieces did not measure up to omnipotent expectations. Matthew Taylor, Jonathan Norton, Samuel Ellington, and Brendan Daltrow, all found out that one of the chief difficulties that obstructed good work patterns was omnipotence, consisting of all-too-high expectations with regard to finished work products and of too much preoccupation with the reactions of others to their work. In all four cases significant changes occurred with ratings ranging from 6 to 9. As the artists returned to the original motivation that had lead them to work, namely sublimation and especially the creation of new objects, they once again focused on work rather than on "audience reactions." The immediate result was increased productivity.

The capacity for oscillation between a state of ego control and of ego loosening or ego regression was maintained in all cases, and in fact in the case of Tina Mandell the capacity was greatly enlarged. Before treatment any regressive experience was felt to be threatening since the artist equated it with insanity. Only after treatment had progressed could she permit herself the self-willed ego regression which is one of the basic conditions for creative work. In the case of Matthew Taylor (Case 1), Jonathan Norton (Case 2) and Brendan Daltrow (Case 6) analytic psychotherapy was most conducive to facilitating regression. Before psychotherapy, repression and affect constriction were extremely severe. Apart from other difficulties which these artists had and which are described in detail, they were blocked in the true sense of the word: their emotions and impulses and imaginative creations could not break forth. All three described themselves as tight. Nothing burst forth when they willed the regressive process to set in. As therapy progressed, communication with their own unconscious improved greatly.

Improved Human Relations Preserve Creative Energy

As to relationships with other human beings, all our artists improved. This did not detract from their ability to settle down to creative work. Quite the contrary was true. As they got along better with wives, sweethearts, employers, etc. more energy was freed to pursue creative work. In other words, it is untrue that an artist has to be unhappy in his or her personal life in order to summon sufficient energy to create. Greater ease in human relations added to and did not detract from the creative effort.

As stated in the beginning the concept of an extra low threshold for stimulation in the creative person only took shape during the development of the project. We possess no measurement as to the nature of the threshold either at the beginning or at the end of therapy. Therapy did not concern itself specifically with changing the nature of the threshold. Therefore we can only suggest that future studies deal with this question. It appears likely, however, both from the facts collected in this study and from facts collected in the treatment of other creative persons, that the artist does face the world with an innate, and thus probably unchangeable, accessibility to stimuli of all kinds.

Most of the artists whom we observed and treated were inordinately passive when they entered treatment. Their passivity gave way to greater activity and assertion as the various ratings clearly show. In every case where passivity gave way to activity work patterns were affected positively.

It should be pointed out again that the study, in particular the sections on changes of work patterns, shows clearly that the much-quoted work block is by no means the only problem that the creative person encounters. Rather there are a great many varieties of difficulties present, as a detailed study of this report clearly shows.

Preliminary Findings to be Tested on Larger Samples

In all cases the triple method of prediction-questionnaires-direction of development ratings revealed certain connections between specific personality problems and work pattern flaws. Nearly every case shows connections to exist between repressed aggression, on the one hand, and lethargy, depression, and stalling in work, on the other hand. In our cases the therapists' concentrating on the inhibition of aggression, and achieving a freeing of aggression helped the patients acquire more effective work patterns. Another connection observed (for instance in the case of Samuel Ellington, page 000) was between super-ego demands and work out-put. The artist patient, who connected his success as a writer with the fulfillment of many omnipotent fantasies, felt guilty whenever he approached success. He then felt compelled to conjure up punishment of one kind or another, to atone beforehand for the anticipated success. A reduction of omnipotent fantasies brought about an amelioration of superego demands and in turn made it possible for the writer to approach work directly without intermediate self-imposed pitfalls. Again this connection between a personality factor and a work pattern problem could be followed up in larger samples of artists.

We found that where work was primarily motivated by a need for rebellion, as in the case of Brendan Daltrow (p. 222) the work patterns suffered. Interestingly enough when this motivation abated, others came into play. Again it will be worthwhile to establish whether this specific connection between a personality factor and the work pattern configuration will be borne out in other cases. Many critics and observers of artists seem to feel that rebellion nurses rather than detracts from the work potential. The observations of Cases 1, 2, 3, 5 and 6 do not bear this out. In these artist patients work patterns improved as rebelliousness against primary figures and society subsided.

As stated in Chapter 2 we elicited questionnaire data separately from the therapists at four-month intervals and from the patients at four-month intervals. The therapists reported on changes in personality proper, the patients on changes in attitudes toward creative work. It was found that a high coincidence existed between the two sources of information. Furthermore, the patients were aware in about 70 per cent of the instances of change in work patterns just what personality changes had lead to specific work changes. This was not due to explicit explanations by the therapists. The therapists did not point out or announce that a release of aggression would help the patient thrust himself more directly and without stalling into work. The patients themselves made this connection.

In summary, the study should give us a basis for predicting that analytic psychotherapy, in addition to improving the patient's subjective feelings about life and putting him into better contact with the world, will help him tackle his work more directly, and effectively.

Bibliography

1. Bellak, Leo: Creativity, Some Random Notes to a Systematic Consideration. *Joural of Projective Techniques,* 22: No. 4, 1958.
2. Bychowski, Gustav: Metapsychology of Artistic Creation. *The Psychoanalytic Quarterly,* XX:599, Oct. 1951.
3. Deutsch, Felix: Mind, Body and Art. *Daedalus,* 89:34, 1960.
4. Freud, Sigmund: Instincts and Their Vicissitudes, *Coll. Papers,* IV.
5. Kris, Ernst: *Psychoanalytic Explorations in Arts.* New York, 1952. International Universities Press.
6. Meerloo, Joost: Vincent Van Gogh's Quest For Identity. *Netherlands Yearbook for History of Art 1964.* Bussum, Holland.
7. Naumburg, Margaret: *Schizophrenic Art: The Meaning in Psychotherapy,* New York, Crane & Stratton, 1950.
8. Sterba and Sterba, Edith and Richard: The Anxieties of Michelangelo Buenaroti. *International Journal of Psychoanalysis,* 37:325-329, 1956.
9. Sykes, Gerald: *The Hidden Remnant.* 1962, p. 16, Harper and Bros.

Index

A

Actor, case report, 98f
Actor-Singer, 98
  acting as means to obtain nurtur-
    ance, 109
  acting skills used to elicit counter
    transference, 108
  and repression of affect, 116
Art teaching, 60, 61, 76, 86, 156
Artist
  and Bohemian, 9
  and human relations, 4
  definition of artist subjects, 10
  personal uniqueness of, 5
Artistic community, 66, 74
  collaboration with, 111
  competition with, 108
  jealousy of, 100
Artistic derivativeness
  and impact of colleagues, 60
  and passivity, 45, 48, 112
Artistic form(s)
  and body image, 68
  and defense system, 53, 146
  and free association, 74
  and identification, 83
  and love of objects, 82
  and partial use of canvas, 74
  and sexual guilt, 54
  and sexual orientation, 46, 48, 126
  change of size of, 72
  emergence of, 65, 142
  vascillation between, 64
Artistic identity, 65, 130f
  and aggression, 62
  and guilt, 67
  and identity, 74
  and indecision, 63

and mechanisms of identification,
  83
  lack of, 126
Artistic motivation, 161
  change in other directedness, 117,
    157
  of painter, 155f, 161
  of sculptor, 45f
  of writer, 126f, 135
Artistic output, 63, 69f, 132, 142
  and anxiety, 46
  and compulsivity, 132
  and conflict, 66, 69f, 159
  and hostility, 66, 152
  and lack of continuity, 62
  and rebelliousness, 135, 155
Artistic productivity
  and aggression, 13, 159
  and anality, 139
  and anxiety, 82, 87, 89, 93, 113
  and concentration, 71
  and discipline, 99
  and ideas of reference, 119
  and infantile fears, 45, 47
  and insanity, 3, 4, 94
  and negativism, 46
  and neurosis, 3, 45, 62, 88, 89, 127
  and oedipus situation, 102, 103
  and other directedness, 100, 126
  and private life, 87, 127
  and secrecy, 96
Artistic products
  and pathology, 6
  and reverberation, 5
  and universality, 5
  changes of, 3, 52f, 128
Artistic rigidity, 43, 143, 159
  and intellectualization, 46